Zola's Son Excellence Eugène Rougon

ZOLA'S

Son Excellence Eugène Rougon

An historical
and critical study by
Richard B. Grant

Duke University Press
Durham, N. C.   1960

Printed in the United States of America
by the Seeman Printery, Durham, North Carolina

To my father.

Acknowledgments

I wish to thank Dr. Jacques Emile-Zola for his gracious permission to quote from the unpublished parts of the manuscript worksheets for Emile Zola's novels. I would also like to take this opportunity to express my gratitude to the Duke University Research Council for its generous grant-in-aid which has made possible the publication of this study.

Table of Contents

Zola's Son Excellence Eugène Rougon

[Chapter One]

The Political Novel before Zola

𝒲e have long been familiar with the
novel which espouses a certain sociopolitical viewpoint. As
examples, Upton Sinclair's *The Jungle,* Victor Hugo's *Les
Misérables* and Tolstoy's *Anna Karenina* are Socialistic, Republican, and Conservative respectively. Yet despite the insistence of these and other authors in upholding a given
political principle, the action of the novels generally takes place
far from any congress or legislature. Once in a while a novel
touches on the process of political selection, such as Booth
Tarkington's *Gentleman from Indiana* or Zola's less well-
known *La Conquête de Plassans;* but in each of these stories
politics is not the whole novel. Tarkington, for instance, is
giving us above all a humorous *étude de mœurs,* and Zola is
examining clerical intrigue in a small town. The true politi-

cal novel is rather uncommon. It deals centrally with politics
and election to a legislature and with the attempt of elected
officials to maintain their power. Such a novel is nearly always based on historical fact and therefore can be considered
as a special form of the historical novel. In nineteenth-century France it reached its ultimate expression in Emile Zola's
Son Excellence Eugène Rougon (1876). Since that time,
it has largely been abandoned by serious French writers who,
if they were realists, turned more to the problem of war, that
haunting specter of the twentieth century. Perhaps too,
authors have felt that contemporary politics, with its pressure
groups and compromises, makes the legislator or political
figure too much of a puppet. The opportunity today for the
rise of a dominant figure might seem at first glance to be in-
creasingly restricted. Personal handouts are nearly a thing
of the past; relief bureaus, staffed with college-trained ad-
ministrators, have weakened the politician's power; civil
service examinations have been killing the spoils system.
Bureaucracy is triumphant in Britain, in France, and in the
United States. Yet the day of the lone figure is not gone.
Only recently a McCarthy could build up tremendous personal power. In France such striking figures as De Gaulle
might inspire a fine literary work.[1] It therefore seems likely
that despite the contemporary emphasis on the metaphysical
novel, we have not heard the last of its more pedestrian
cousin.

While the basic struggle to reach or maintain power is
by definition at the heart of the political novel, its setting
must reflect the form of government of the period about
which it was written. In nineteenth-century France the legislature first emerged as a genuine reality after the Revolution

---

[1] In the United States novels by Robert Penn Warren, *All the King's
Men* (1946), and Edwin O'Connor, *The Last Hurrah* (1956), indicate
contemporary interest in the political novel on this side of the Atlantic.

of 1830. It was only natural, therefore, that the writers of the first third of the century either did not notice, or perhaps did not care to become involved in, the new reality of their age. They also lacked the distance necessary to bring it into proper focus. It is not surprising, then, to find Alfred de Vigny, in 1827, looking deep into the past for his "political novel," which *Cinq-Mars* is, in a certain sense. Vigny's central thesis, that Richelieu's destruction of the power of the nobility was harmful to France in that it destroyed the balance of power and created an overcentralized government, makes *Cinq-Mars* more than just an ordinary historical novel. It attempts, though only partially, to seek out and to study the mechanism of the nation's power structure, and then to judge it. But because Vigny does not have any real legislature or politician to study, this novel is only an interesting precursor.

Vigny's attempt at analysis and judgment would, however, also be true of the real political novel of the nineteenth century. It was here that Zola was to encounter a serious problem: how to reconcile the objectivity of the realistic or naturalistic author with the desire to criticize some regime or system of government which is inevitably found in all political novels.

Stendhal represented a step forward. He wrote openly of contemporary events, choosing the Bourbon Restoration for *Le Rouge et le Noir* and Italy after 1815 for *La Chartreuse de Parme*. In the former novel he merely suggested the political struggles of that era. Stendhal's love of dashing intrigue and his hatred of the mediocre kept him far from any Chamber of Deputies. He concentrated instead on the fierce but secret battles of the Congregation and conservatives against any form of liberalism. He was preoccupied by the nature of power, but chose not to enter into the political arena as

such. *La Chartreuse de Parme* also reflects this point of view.
It has been said that this novel is an attempt to fuse nineteenth-
century reality in Italy with the spirit of the Renaissance.
Stendhal of course preferred the latter, but was obliged
to have Count Mosca, who was wondering about a career of
some kind for the aristocratic Fabrice, exclaim ruefully, "Le
siècle est aux avocats." There seemed to be no more place for
bravura in the modern world. The last outposts were the
small Italian states which were ruled by intrigue. Stendhal
had brushed up against the political world, but except where
he concerned himself with secret maneuvering, he turned
away from it.

It was inevitably Balzac who first tried to come to grips
with modern politics, which were for him the regimes of the
Bourbon Restoration, and later, the July Monarchy. But
he was interested in characters and in life in society to such
an extent that he tended to go behind what he considered
to be the political façade and seek the truth of financial and
class antagonisms. Balzac saw clearly that the political power
was in the hands of the monarchy prior to 1830. He saw
also that this regime, which had come back into power largely
through foreign efforts, was not only living in the past, but
was also suffering from hardened arteries. The government
functioned largely by means of momentum inherited from the
past, and routine work done by office clerks. This transi-
tional period in French government Balzac analyzed bril-
liantly in separate works. *La Duchesse de Langeais* (1833)
is a severe criticism of the politics of the Faubourg Saint-
Germain. The nobility was defeated in 1830 because it had
lost contact with reality, that is, with the nation. The
aristocrats were absorbed in their own sterile egotism. Similarly in *Illusions Perdues,* Balzac describes at some length

the former pre-eminence of the nobility, and comes to the same conclusion:

Angoulême est une vieille ville bâtie au sommet d'une roche en pain de sucre. . . . L'importance qu'avait cette ville au temps des guerres religieuses est attestée par ses remparts, par ses portes et par les restes d'une forteresse assise sur le piton du rocher . . . . mais sa force d'autrefois constitue sa faiblesse d'aujourd'hui; en empêchant de s'étaler, ses remparts et la pente trop rapide du rocher l'ont condamnée à la plus funeste immobilité.

Meanwhile, at the foot of the hill, the business area was prospering and expanding, making two cities in one.

Le faubourg de l'Houmeau devint donc une ville industrielle et riche . . . que jalouse la ville haute où restent le Gouvernement, l'Évêché, la Justice, l'Aristocratie." In this upper city "la plupart des maisons . . . sont habitées ou par des familles bourgeoises qui vivent de leurs revenus et composent une sorte de nation autochtone dans laquelle les étrangers ne sont jamais reçus . . . . Moqueuses, dénigrantes, jalouses, avares, ces maisons marient entre elles, se forment un bataillon serré pour ne laisser ni sortir ni entrer personne; les créations de luxe moderne elles les ignoraient; pour elles, envoyer un enfant à Paris, c'est vouloir le perdre.[2]

Balzac looked into the bureaucracy that kept France running regardless of political regime in *Les Employés* (1836). This volume is a detailed examination of the strugles for promotion within the various bureaus. There are the inevitable opposing groups, and the ultimate victor is supported by the clergy. The emphasis here, however, is far more upon personalities. The honest Xavier Rabourdin, thanks to a tactical error or two, is cheated out of a legitimate and well-earned promotion by a rival of absolute nullity. In the last analysis, this triumph of the asinine is due to the

[2] Balzac, *Oeuvres complètes,* ed. Bouteron and Longnon (Paris, 1913), XI, 204-206.

senility of the nation's leaders. For Balzac, energy is essential, and age does not possess it. The novelist admires the youthful Napoleon who was able to accomplish miracles by tapping this reservoir, by putting eager young men into positions of responsibility. The Bourbons gave the reins of government over to the septuagenarians of the peerage, who were too tired to want anything but the status quo and too stupid to rely on Talleyrand's genius. Hence, as a cynical character of *Les Employés* remarks, Rabourdin (who wished to introduce sweeping reforms) will lose because he has exceptional creative qualities and his opponent does not. Such cynicism was largely justified.

To Balzac's mind, the future lay with the energetic men of the nineteenth century. In his novels these are the financiers, the Nucigens, the Kellers. It also lay in the hands of the businessmen. If César Birotteau succumbed, his son-in-law Anselme Popinot emerged as a source of wealth and power for the future. These are the people who commanded Balzac's admiration. He was less interested by the politicians in the Chamber of Deputies, first because he had had no real contact with them and he tended to write only of things he knew, and secondly because they seemed to him to represent only extensions of the power of others.

Having gained what he felt was a clear idea of the sources of power, Balzac created one volume, *Scènes de la Vie Politique,* to take its place in *La Comédie Humaine.* Curiously, the first of the three tales that comprise this volume, *Une Ténébreuse affaire* (1841), is not a "political novel" at all, but a return to the historical novel of intrigue. The scene is the First Empire, when what we know today as politics was hardly possible under Napoleon's firm control. The plot concerns various attempts at conspiracy against the Emperor. The only visible reason for including it

in a collection of political tales would seem to be that it
gives the background for the next tale, *Le Député d'Arcis,*
which can truly be called the first attempt at a political novel
among the important writers of the century.

It is significant that this half-novel (Balzac never finished
it) did not appear until 1847. It took a full generation of
genuine representative government for the novelists to catch
up with its existence, and by this date France had had many
years of the constitutional monarchy of Louis-Philippe.
The structure of this work is tortuous. The novel is marred
by many explanations of what had happened in the past.
There can be no denying that it is in general an inferior
piece of writing, with only occasional flashes of brilliance.
But stripped of many unessential side issues, the plot becomes
fairly simple. The district of Arcis-sur-Aube, having been
a "rotten borough" for some time, becomes restive in 1839;
and, many of its citizens, in order to assert their political in-
dependence, wish to repudiate the wealthy and powerful
Keller family, although as deputies to the Chamber of Deputies the Kellers had done well by the district. The Keller
running for office this year is the handsome and dashing
Charles, a brave officer, dedicated to the government of
Louis-Philippe. Nonetheless, a strong movement in favor of
young and mediocre Simon Giguet gives the entrenched
powers some anxiety, but they feel, probably correctly, that
the community will not really be so foolish as to elect him.
Shortly before the election Charles Keller is killed in Africa.
The government in Paris, fearful that the seat may pass over
to the opposition, decides to send a man to Arcis-sur-Aube
to defeat Giguet. This new man is none other than that old
roué Maxime de Trailles, who is desirous of settling down.
De Trailles goes incognito to Arcis to begin his campaign.

The reader gains the impression that De Trailles will win. It is at this point that Balzac ceased writing.

The message of *Le Député d'Arcis* is fairly clear. As of 1839, representative democracy was not yet a genuine achievement. The government in Paris could, by exerting its influence, very often determine the outcome of an election. The people had only an illusion of power. But Balzac, through Rastignac, foresees the day when the Chamber will be a mighty force. "Il y a un combat, plus violent que le vulgaire ne le croit, entre une puissance au maillot et une puissance enfant. La puissance au maillot, c'est la Chambre des Députés, qui n'étant pas contenue par une chambre héréditaire . . . deviendra fatalement tout le gouvernement . . . . La puissance enfant est la royauté couronnée au mois d'août 1830."[3] For the moment, however, there is only illusion of government by the people.

This insistence on the duplicity ever present in political affairs is at the core of the earlier *Z. Marcas* (1840), which closes the *Scènes de la Vie Politique*. Marcas tells a group of students of his own failure as a politician. He was a profoundly learned lawyer; he was a fine orator. He knew the Chamber of Deputies. In fact, he was the perfect model of what a statesman should be. He was quick of action and penetrating in his judgments. But he was poor. Therefore, he tried to rise to power by working for a wealthy, ambitious, and stupid deputy. It was here that his decency betrayed him. He was too fine a person, and the man whom he helped rise to the top was just intelligent enough to realize Marcas' ambitions, and betrayed him. Marcas came to be considered dangerous. Calumny destroyed him. He planned to emigrate, and urged the young students to do the same. The advice recalls Balzac's earlier lament in *Les*

[3] *Ibid.,* XXI, 395-396.

Employés. A righteous, practical, able person in government
will succumb to the petty assaults of the envious mediocrities.
While in *Le Député d'Arcis,* the town will perhaps be conquered by the powerful, intelligent, and unscrupulous (Rastignac and de Trailles), in general the victories in Balzac go
in politics to the nullities, persistent as worms digging
through the soil. Thus authors as dissimilar as Vigny,
Stendhal, and Balzac all feared the triumph of mediocrity as
a consequence of giving the vote to the bourgeoisie.[4] Zola,
coming a generation after Balzac, would have the examples
of these predecessors to ponder, and he too suspected that the
crawling mediocrity of the spoils-seekers would effectively
challenge the daring of the clever and unscrupulous.

[4] Flaubert, having taken refuge in the Temple of Art, had little use
for the pettiness of politics, and if in *Education sentimentale* Frédéric
Moreau half-heartedly runs for office in 1848, Flaubert has him do so
only in an attempt to show the utter futility of the youth's effort.

[Chapter Two]

Genesis and Composition

$\mathscr{S}on$ *Excellence Eugène Rougon* remains today one of the least known of Emile Zola's novels, no doubt because the great themes of life and death, fecundity and sterility, which give epic power to such novels as *Germinal* and *La Terre,* are intentionally subordinated to the petty squabbles of sordid politicians.[1]   Yet a political novel certainly should not be considered as extraneous to the over-all concept of the *Rougon-Macquart* series.   Quite the contrary, from the very beginning Zola had planned to include a genuine political novel as part of his study of the Second Empire.

[1] Maurice LeBlond in his critical commentary at the end of the (so-called) Bernouard edition (pp. 407-408) reminds us that the novel was forgotten in the storm raised by the publication of *L'Assommoir,* which began appearing in *Le Bien Public* a few weeks after the publication of *Son Excellence Eugène Rougon.* All future quotations from Zola's writings are from this edition.

A brief summary of the first idea for this novel can be found in his original plans submitted in 1868 to the editor Lacroix. Here he writes of

un roman qui aura pour cadre le monde officiel et pour héros Alfred Goiraud [i.e., Eugène Rougon], l'homme qui a aidé au coup d'état. Je puis en faire soit un ministre, soit un grand fonctionnaire. L'ambition d'Alfred est plus haute que celle des autres membres de la famille. Il a moins soif d'argent que de puissance. Mais le sens de la justice lui manque; il est un digne soutien de l'empire.[2]

It is already clear from the last sentence that the novelist, despite his scientific pretentions, was far from impartial. The naturalist might disclaim any satirical intent when drawing up his plans for the *Rougon-Macquart*: "Je ne veux pas établir ou défendre une politique ou une religion. Mon étude est un simple coin d'analyse du monde tel qu'il est. Je constate purement."[3] Zola even went so far as to write in his "Différences entre Balzac et moi" that he chose the background of the Second Empire "uniquement pour créer un milieu qui réagisse."[4] But when he started the *ébauche* for *Son Excellence Eugène Rougon,* he quickly revealed the truth, writing: "on peut faire ainsi de l'œuvre une splendide satire."[5] This hostile viewpoint was of course nothing new

[2] Quoted from the manuscript worksheets (on deposit at the Bibliothèque nationale). Nouvelles acquisitions françaises (hereinafter referred to as N.A.F.), 10304, *feuillet* 55. Reproduced in LeBlond, after *La Fortune des Rougon,* pp. 359-360.

[3] Quoted from the extracts of Zola's preliminary notes to the *Rougon-Macquart* at the end of *La Fortune des Rougon,* p. 354.

[4] N.A.F. 10345, *f.* 15. Cited by LeBlond, *La Fortune des Rougon,* p. 357.

[5] N.A.F. 10292 (the notes for *Son Excellence Eugène Rougon*), f. 98. F.W.J. Hemmings in his *Emile Zola* (Oxford, 1953) pp. 52 *et seq.* considers the problem of the naturalist's scientific objectivity and his condemnation of the Second Empire, concluding rightly that the synthesis was an uneasy one, with the polemical side dominating. This is particularly true for *La Curée,* for example, but as we shall see in the case of this

with Zola. In his prefatory "Notes sur la marche générale
de l'œuvre" he wrote bluntly: "L'Empire a déchaîné les
appétits et les ambitions. Orgie d'appétits et d'ambition.
Soif de jouir et de jouir par la pensée surmenée et le corps
surmené."[6] Indeed from the very first novel, Zola began
a systematic exposé of the defects of that regime. In *La
Fortune des Rougon* he pictured the brutal repression of the
decent Republicans, and also hinted at the unscrupulous campaign of Bonapartist propaganda in the provinces prior to
the coup d'état of December, 1851. In *La Curée,* the political
world is less important than that of high society. Behind the
glitter of the festivities and the feverish transformation of
Paris under Baron Haussmann, there lies a world of intrigue
where, for example, the politically powerful Eugène Rougon
favors his brother Aristide not only with a job, but also with
an opportunity to make a killing in speculating on the expro-
priation of buildings. Here too men try to buy their way
into the *Corps législatif.*[7] In *Le Ventre de Paris,* the efficient
operation of the Imperial police squelches a conspiracy, and
finally in *La Conquête de Plassans,* we watch the elections
of 1863, with the pro-Bonapartist priest sent by the Ministry
of the Interior in Paris to combat the Ultramontane clergy
which was supporting the Orleanists and Legitimists. But
all these details, accurate as they are as examples of political
activity under the Second Empire, remain peripheral and
fragmentary. A novel treating the political nerve-center was
needed. Zola did not delay long. *Son Excellence Eugène
Rougon,* which he had finished in early September, 1875,[8]

political novel, Zola was able to be satirical without betraying historical
truth unduly.
    [6] Reproduced at the end of *La Fortune des Rougon,* pp. 353-355.
    [7] Cf. *La Curée,* p. 130.
    [8] A letter dated September 8, 1875 states that he has just finished
the novel. *Correspondance, 1872-1902,* p. 434.

ran in thirty-five instalments in *Le Siècle* from January 25, 1876, to March 11 of that year. It was issued in book form by Charpentier the same month.

As was his custom, Zola started his preparation for the novel without any fixed plot. He was armed with a character and above all with a central idea. The very first *feuillet* of the notes is labeled *Plan* and strikes out boldly with the basic theme:

L'ambition d'un homme qui idolâtre sa force et son intelligence.
Les Coulisses politiques. Les affaires dites sérieuses.
La vilenie, la bassesse, l'ignorance, la vénalité. Et la passion changeant les hommes en loups.
Historie d'un parti, d'une coterie, poussant son chef et le dévorant. L'empire, beau champignon de despotisme poussé en pleine société démocrate.[9]

These basic ideas are repeated in more elaborate form at the very beginning of the *ébauche,* and foreshadow the general movement of the final text. Hence one can see that documentation was to support a pre-established idea, not to lead to it.[10]

Next Zola sought a story. After making a rapid survey of the *Rougon-Macquart* characters who were living in Paris in the late 1850's, the novelist quickly decided to select as his protagonist Eugène Rougon, the former caseless lawyer of Plassans, who had risen to power in *La Curée.* He would appear as a strong, ambitious man who rises to the top and becomes the Minister of State. But he would be worn down in the end, eaten up by the members of his own band who compromise him with their unquenchable thirst for loot: "lui, si fort, supérieur, rongé . . . anéanti"[11]—and Zola added: "C'est l'histoire des gouvernements." Thus at this point

[9] N.A.F. 10292.   [10] *Cf.* below, pp. 20-21.
[11] N.A.F. 10292, *f.* 99.

we have the prospect of a completely pessimistic ending. But
so far Zola had sketched only the general movement, not the
human drama, and he mused: "Maintenant il me faut un
drame là-dessus, si petit qu'il soit."[12] The main interest would
still be, he hoped, in the twenty or so little episodes in which
the members of the band succeed in getting what they want,
but Zola recognized the need for "un but d'action centrale."[13]

It was apparently at this point, after some hesitation,
that he found the key to his novel: the beautiful Italian
adventuress (Clorinde Balbi) who would lead the opposition
against Rougon and succeed in overthrowing him. For a
long time, however, Zola seemed unable to decide which of
his two main characters should emerge triumphant. We have
already seen that the first idea was for Rougon to end
"anéanti, rongé par sa bande." The adventuress had not yet
been thought of. Yet having decided upon Rougon's ultimate
defeat, he added as an afterthought: "avec une revanche de
son esprit supérieur à la fin." Despite the possible ambiguity
of this phrase which might lead one to believe that Zola
was planning Rougon's final triumph, the meaning seems
to be that the politician's revenge would be verbal only, that
it would consist merely of some final cutting comment. As
Zola developed the picture, Rougon is clearly the loser. At
first all would go well with him. He would conquer and
possess Clorinde and even marry her to one of his henchmen,
using her as a political tool to defeat a rival in power. But
for Zola voluptuous women were more than untrustworthy.
She would commit "une canaillerie énorme," pass over to
the opposition and put her idiotic husband on the top of the
heap.[14] The novel would end with her crushing comment:

[12] *F.* 103. Quoted by LeBlond, p. 413 of *SEER.*
[13] *Ibid.*
[14] *F.* 106. ". . . renverse mon ministre pour placer son imbécile de
mari à son poste."

"Vous aviez raison, dit-elle à mon ministre, nous nous serions battus,[15] tandis que maintenant je règne seule." But such a plan for the novel's structure left Zola dissatisfied. He wrote uneasily (*f.* 106) : "Quelque chose de plus net et de plus fin à trouver." Why? He does not say, and therefore we must speculate on the problem of his self-association with his characters. Zola was a hammerer, a man who by sheer will power conquered the literary world of the last part of the nineteenth century despite the open hostility of the official critics. In his novels, when a bull-like character of strong will appears,[16] he is usually chaste and fearful of woman, who represents the enemy of man's will. It seems that Zola felt somewhat the same way until his liaison with Jeanne Rozerot.[17] Consequently, while Rougon is a scoundrel, he appears to have Zola's admiration for being one of the few men who do not succumb to the fatal charm of sex. (One has but to turn the pages of *Nana* to watch the ordinary flies being devoured by the spider.) It would be reasonable to guess that the novelist felt a certain masculine solidarity with his male character, and would prefer to see him triumph over the female. Furthermore, the dramatic intensity of the novel would be heightened by a battle in which the male did not fall too easily.

Nonetheless, Zola continued to accept momentarily the defeat of Rougon and even modified his relationship with Clorinde. He would fail to possess her: "Elle couche avec tout le monde sauf avec mon ministre.[18] Piquant. Mon

---

[15] If they had married.

[16] E.g., Faujas in *La Conquête de Plassans,* frère Archangias in *La Faute de l'Abbé Mouret.*

[17] Hemmings, p. 71, and Angus Wilson, *Emile Zola: An Introductory Study of His Novels* (New York, 1952), *passim,* have developed this idea considerably.

[18] Zola sums up the characteristics of his adventuress (*f.* 118) : "En somme, très femme, très souple, ni bonne, ni mauvaise, comme toujours; la vie étudiée sans parti pris."

ministre pourra dire 'J'aurais dû être général.' Ou peut-être prendra-t-il sa revanche d'un mot" (ƒ. 106). He leaves the problem there for the time being, referring later on (ƒ. 114) to this same defeat: "Tout en haut la grande intelligence d'Eugène planant et dominant, jusqu'au jour où il sera roulé par une femme et par sa clique."

At the same time that Zola was slowly elaborating this basic duel between man and woman, he was also preoccupied with the political picture. He of course had a general knowledge of the years from 1852 to 1870. He had lived through them and had been a journalist. In his preparation for *La Fortune des Rougon,* he had even consulted historical works. Thus, in the *ébauche,* Zola wrote easily and naturally of the basic facts and personalities of the Second Empire. In order to situate his novel and to provide a political drama, he finally decided[19] to place this story during the change from the authoritarian rule of 1852-60 to the so-called Liberal Empire of the next decade, but well before 1869, when the Empire did, in fact, remove most of the restrictions on personal liberty: "Je prends comme nœud une velléité d'empire libéral avant 69."[20] At this time he had the idea of writing two political novels, dividing the Empire chronologically into parts.[21] The other political novel was never written, as such. In an intermediate list of his novels, which must date from about this time (published in *La Fortune des Rougon,* p. 361), Zola referred to a "deuxième roman sur le peuple, particulièrement politique," which would be *Germinal,* and a "roman sur la guerre, le siège et la commune," which is of course *La Débâcle.* But in these two novels the political aspects become subordinated to other considerations,

[19] Cf. ƒ. 116; cited in LeBlond edition, p. 415.
[20] *F.* 114; LeBlond, p. 415.
[21] *F.* 122: "Je crois qu'il est préférable puisque j'ai deux romans à faire sur la politique de scinder l'empire en deux."

and *Son Excellence Eugène Rougon* remains his only true political novel. But because of this initial desire to leave room for another one, Zola, after some hesitation,[22] moved his story into the late 1850's, planning to end it in 1860 or in 1861, with the proclamation of the Liberal Empire.[23]

Meanwhile, Zola had been struggling with the problem of the blocs of power that would confront each other, paying particular attention to Rougon's rival. His first idea, as Rougon was to be an authoritarian strong-man, was to take Napoleon III's somewhat liberal views and incarnate them in some fictional cabinet member who would be dreaming of "humanitairerie" (*f.* 100). But then he decided to postpone this version until the second political novel. Whoever the rival might be, however, he too would have his clique— "sa meute"—(*f.* 113). The naturalist imagined hastily what jobs each of these hangers-on might have, but decided to leave these faceless men "beaucoup plus dans l'ombre," obviously to avoid overpopulating his novel. The purpose would not be to create characters, but rather "ce qu'il faut, c'est opposer les deux catégories, animer le drame par leur rivalité; bien montrer sous le large courant des intérêts gouvernementaux et sociaux, la bataille des intérêts personnels." Zola insisted on this turbulence, writing (*f.* 114): "Il faut que tout cela soit très grouillant," and he even went so far as to add (*f.* 118): "Je chercherai moins que jamais à raconter une histoire."

Coming back to the battle between the two politicians, Zola first made it clear how much Eugène Rougon despises the Empire, the Emperor, and all liberalism. His desire is

[22] Cf. *f.* 189.
[23] "Dans le premier roman j'étudierai l'époque de 52 à 60, le silence dans la chambre, avec l'indication du réveil de l'opposition en 57. Dans l'autre [also mentioned *f.* 100] j'étudierai les réformes libérales de 60 jusqu'à l'avènement du ministère Ollivier en 70." *F.* 122.

to be alone, to govern alone, but he, too, must have a coterie if he wishes to succeed. "Son Morny, son Billault, son Persigny, son Saint-Arnaud; et ce sera sa coterie qui le noiera. Garder comme type la bande du deux décembre" (*f.* 115). As to the rival, he will now be a mixture of the Emperor, with his social and democratic dreams, and of Emile Ollivier (*f.* 115). But Ollivier, though no genius, was a reasonably honest man, and in this novel there would be little place at the top for such a person. Therefore, Zola wrote longingly (*f.* 119): "J'aurais désiré y mettre le type du duc de Morny. Mais je ne vois pas trop le moyen." His adventuress, he mused, might be his mistress on her way to the top, but Zola abandoned this speculation with his customary "tous ces détails sont à fixer." (*f.* 119).

At this stage in the development of the novel, Zola had not yet turned to direct documentation from the historians. It is only at *feuillet* 120 that he paused to take stock and decided:

Il me faut maintenant

     1) Prendre les notes sur la politique pour fixer le drame politique

     2) arrêter les intrigues secondaires . . . .

     3) Faire un plan détaillé . . . .

     4) Prendre les notes sur la Ch. [ambre] et les ministères.

This step was necessary, for if, like any citizen, he had some basic knowledge of what the Empire had been, not much of it was very precise. And we know that it was at this moment that he actually did stop to read history, for the very next *feuillet* contains phrases and facts directly traceable to his sources.

We are therefore in a position to draw nearly the same conclusion concerning *Son Excellence Eugène Rougon* that

Professor Guy Robert did for *La Terre* : that the general in-
spiration and direction of the novel was clearly established
prior to the famed "documentation." This should come as
no surprise in the case of an historical novel, for, as we have
already mentioned, he had documented himself politically for
earlier novels, and had lived through much of the era in
question. He thus had the necessary fund of knowledge to
set the general lines of his new book prior to making a detailed study. Yet this new documentation was vital because
it would give Zola many incidents, many scenes for the novel.
It would even alter slightly his interpretation of the policies
of the Empire and aid him in situating the novel prior to
1861, because that decision, as we have seen, is noted on
feuillet 122.

What were Zola's historical sources? Georges Lote, in
his "Zola, historien du second Empire," states clearly that
not only did the novelist utilize the six-volume work (five
had appeared before 1875) of the Republican historian
Taxile Delord,[24] but that in addition, he followed the structure of Delord's work and patterned his novel after it.[25]
F.W.J. Hemmings likewise gives Delord as the main source
for the political background.[26] Now there is no question
that Zola knew and used Delord's history. He had consulted
it for one of the earlier novels,[27] and also referred to it in
his notes for *Son Excellence Eugène Rougon* (f. 190). Hemmings observed (p. 58) that Zola gave an extract from the

[24] *Histoire du second Empire (1848-1869)* (Paris, 1869-1875), 6 vols.
[25] *Revue des études napoléoniennes,* juillet-août, 1918, p. 81.
[26] P. 58.
[27] The manuscript notes from Delord are to be found in the back of
of the notes for *SEER,* but should properly be included, judging from
their content concerning early Bonapartist propaganda and from the hand-
writing which is of Zola's early period, probably with the notes for *La
Fortune des Rougon,* or conceivably with those for *La Conquête de
Plassans.*

first volume in his second series of "Livres d'aujourd'hui et de demain," written for *Le Gaulois*. Furthermore, it is clear from internal evidence, as we shall see later, that Zola took certain scenes bodily from Delord, although there is no mention of Delord's name in N.A.F. 10292. But Delord is not Zola's most important source. As has been pointed out by Prof. E.M. Grant in his "Studies on Zola's *Son Excellence Eugène Rougon*,"[28] the most important is Ernest Hamel's *Histoire Illustrée du second Empire*. Zola has over twenty pages of notes on Hamel's work (*ff*. 172-193), complete with the page references for his quotations.

It is not difficult to guess why, in general, Zola preferred Hamel to Delord for his basic review of those eighteen years. Hamel's history is shorter, more popular, and even more Republican than Delord's, whose work, incidentally, Hamel undoubtedly used in writing his own; finally Hamel is perhaps easier to read and to take notes on. Of course, both historians tell essentially the same story and in essentially the same way, and were it not for the specific page references to Hamel, it would sometimes be nearly impossible to tell which book Zola utilized for his documentation.

The first evidence of Zola's documentation is clearly on *feuillet* 121 where he refers to material taken from Hamel. We find here the date for the beginning of the novel: "56 à 57 apogée de l'empire."[29] At this time, the country was dutifully obedient to the Emperor and Zola wished to start at that point to show "de quelle façon se brasse[nt] les affaires dites sérieuses" (*f*. 98). His first idea is not to be found in the *ébauche,* but in certain "Notes particulières" (*ff*. 173-176) based on Hamel. He would begin with the

[28] *Romanic Review,* XLIV (1953), 24.
[29] Also *f*. 182, which quotes Hamel on this phrase (II, 199). The expression is also in Delord, II, 2. The notes from Hamel are on *ff*. 172-193.

sum of money voted to Marshal Pélissier in early 1857. Pélissier, who had seized the key forts at Sebastopol and had thus hastened the end of the Crimean War, was made Duke of Malakoff, and on March 27, 1857,[30] at the request of the Emperor, he was granted an annual sum of 100,000 francs, transmissible to direct male heirs. As he was already far from poor, with a Marshal's salary, one might have expected some protests from the *Corps législatif*, all the more so since Pélissier's victory was not a particularly brilliant one. But the yes-men in the Assembly voted the annuity without a dissenting voice. As a starting point for a novel of satirical intent, this was nearly ideal. Zola even copied the speech made in favor of the motion. But as he read on in Hamel, Zola came upon the description of the baptism of the Imperial Prince (June 14, 1856), and he learned too that a 400,000 franc supplement to the budget had been voted in May of that year to defray the expenses of that ceremony. In adopting this episode instead, he could satirize the legislative body even more sharply for squandering money and following the Emperor's whims in slavish fashion, and he would also have the pleasure of describing the event itself, a colorful spectacle with its massed crowds. Thus Zola had finally found a point of departure for this novel. He copied into his notes the text of the speech which proposed the voting of the credits (*ff.* 228-232).

After *f.* 120, the *ébauche* plunges into the specific details of the story that he gleaned from Hamel: an incident of political repression, a railroad swindle, etc. But most important, Zola had found the answer to his final chapter. Although the adventuress, having slept with Rougon's rival,

[30] Zola, *f.* 173, following Hamel, I, 214, refers to the date as Feb. 1857. F. Doucet, *L'Esthétique d'Emile Zola et son application à la critique* (Paris, 1923), p. 198, errs in accepting the statement that the novel begins in February.

has now become the Emperor's mistress, thus succeeding in forcing Eugène's resignation, the latter will have an ultimate political victory:

Maintenant, pour finir par une séance du corps législatif, je puis montrer dans un dernier chapitre Rougon revenant au pouvoir en 1860 comme ministre sans portefeuille; il est devant la chambre, et je montre une grande séance de discussion avec l'opposition. Il aurait le dernier mot, avec mon aventurière, ou du moins je finirai en plein cynisme politique ainsi que j'ai fini dans *La Curée* en plein cynisme moral.[31] Rougon qui a été le représentant terrible de la répression à outrance célèbre les grandeurs de l'empire libéral. Mon aventurière . . . vient le féliciter. Dernier mot sanglant.

Zola concludes:

"D'après ce plan, Rougon devient un véritable ministre de l'empire, sans principe, sans conviction autre que son besoin de pouvoir . . . . Je n'en fais pas un homme d'esprit, mais un homme sans scrupules, affamé de pouvoir, véritablement fort par son besoin de domination. (*f*. 125)

Zola then settled certain minor incidents of the novel (*ff*. 127 *et seq.*). There is the story of some litigation over a Spanish ship which causes Rougon's first fall from power,[32] the incident of political repression, etc. More important, Zola decided to relegate Rougon's political adversary to a minor role, and to replace him with the Woman (*f*. 129):

Eugène Rougon n'a plus de rival. Je garde seulement Morny qui lui est opposé par tempérament et qui le combat . . . . Cela d'ailleurs simplifiera le roman. A la fin, mon Rougon ne voit pas cette femme qui lui tendra un piège pour le faire tomber.

---

[31] The reference is to the servant Baptiste, who seems to be the one virtuous person unmoved by the allure of woman, and by all the evil surrounding him. We learn at the end of the novel that he is a homosexual. Also at the end, Saccard cheerfully accepts his wife's infidelity with his son.

[32] We have been unable to find an historical source for this reference.

Zola had previously concluded (*f.* 118) :

Le roman deviendra ainsi une large page sociale et humaine. J'éviterai un dénouement terrible. Le livre ne se dénouera pas par un drame. Il s'arrêtera quand j'aurai fini. Mais il pourra continuer encore. J'y mettrai plus de souplesse que dans les autres . . . . J'étalerai une simple peinture de caractère et de faits. Cela pourra être d'un grand effet.[33]

There is little evidence so far to show that the novel would become a "vast social and human page." This summary reveals, rather, that Zola was concentrating on the basic form of the book: the mechanism for Rougon's rise and fall. He realized that he would need a basically loose structure.

Feuillet 136 follows the *ébauche* directly and is the first chapter plan that Zola drew up. It seems to have been composed after his reading in Hamel, for the terminal date of 1860-61, with Rougon's change of political skin, is mentioned, and it was no doubt written immediately after the *ébauche* was finished. It is far from the "plan détaillé" that Zola referrred to on *f.* 120; it was left intentionally vague to allow for expansion:

ler chapitre Séance du Corps législatif. Poser mes personnages. L'histoire de la disgrâce de Rougon.

2e chapitre — Les créatures de Rougon autour de lui. Rougon explique son plan. Je pose la meute. Je noue les intrigues secondaires.

3e chapitre — Mon aventurière. Elle tente Rougon. Leurs amours. Il la marie.

4e — La lutte de Rougon et de sa meute pour remonter au pouvoir.

5e chapitre — Rougon au pouvoir. Une scène grandiose.

[33] LeBlond puts this paragraph at the end of his sample of the *ébauche*. In fact, it comes about two-thirds of the way through it.

6ᵉ — Rougon au pouvoir. Mais ébranlé par mon aventurière. Histore de sa chute.

7ᵉ — Le dénouement. La séance au Corps législatif en 1860-1.

One may note from this outline that even though the novelist had by now read about the baptism of the Imperial Prince in Hamel, and about the money voted for the costs of this ceremony, these are not mentioned here. Indeed, it is not until the final chapter plan that they are included. We may therefore conclude that Zola made his final decision for this part of the novel rather late in the day.

In the "plan des chapitres," each of these first chapter headings, except the last one, is elaborated in some detail.[34] The first chapter is to take place in early 1857, with the grant of money to Marshal Pélissier, as Zola first planned. An Imperial party at Compiègne is first mentioned on *f.* 39 (outline for Chapter III). Rougon's political trip to the provinces is sketched (*f.* 57). But it is the absence of the seventh chapter, with Rougon's ultimate triumph, that is of particular interest. Zola has, apparently, suppressed it for the moment. In his plans for the sixth chapter, he projected: "Enfin un dernier chapitre donnant tout un démenti à la conduite de Rougon," (*f.* 57) but he then crossed out this sentence with his pen. Apparently he was still hesitating. We read subsequently on *f.* 66 what will be the pessimistic ending: Rougon is surprised and irritated by his defeat, the woman is overjoyed. The male finally accepts defeat philosophically with a vile insult for the adventuress. This chapter, now the final one, closes as the members of Rougon's band start to attach themselves to the rival.

But even as he was writing this first plan, Zola was thinking out a more elaborate one. On *f.* 6 he had already

[34] Chap. i—*ff.* 6-8; chap. ii—*ff.* 13-16; chap. iii—*f.* 31; chap. iv—*f.* 39; chap. v—*f.* 51; chap. vi—*ff.* 64-66.

foreseen a final total of about fifteen chapters with perhaps about thirty pages each. At the end of the sixth chapter, he refers to the suppressed seventh chapter as the tenth chapter, implying that in addition to restoring the original final chapter, he had three more in mind. In other words, his decision to eliminate the final revenge of Rougon did not last long. There seems no way to explain this temporary elimination unless Zola had been hesitating between utter pessimism (first version) and complete cynicism (final version).

The next chapter outline, which is much more elaborate than the first one, is given on *f. 2*:

mai 56 Chapitre Ier — Le Corps législatif
                II — Le déménagement
juillet 56   III — La visite de Rougon à l'aventurière. Un intérieur de femme excentrique.
——[Là un chapitre dans de cadre du baptême, avec tous les personnages]
sept 56   IV — La scène de la serre.[35] Mariage de l'aventurière.
dec 56 à sept 57 V — Chez Rougon l'été. La conspiration pour le faire remonter au pouvoir. Mariage de Rougon.
——[un autre chapitre sur la conspiration et la politique]
sept 57   VI — Compiègne. On travaille pour Rougon.
jan 58   VII — Le complot. Rougon épousant les querelles et se décidant.
fev 58   VIII — Rougon ministre. Déjeuner avec l'aventurière.
58   IX — Inauguration. Rougon en province. Le drame
                 X — A Paris, une fête officielle (bal, ouverture de Chambre, 15 août, jour de l'an?) L'aventurière ébranlant Rougon. Chute de celui-ci. (Une scène au Sénat)
mars 61   XII — En. 1860. Rougon ministre sans portefeuille. Le cynisme en politique.—Dénouement. Je mettrai là les détails sur la Chambre.

[35] Later changed to a stable, possibly because he had already used a greenhouse in *La Curée*.

—Voir un chapitre sur les élections de (57).
Le Sénat, avec l'ancien amant de la comtesse Balbi.

This outline shows quite clearly that the details for the novel were thought out in nearly definitive form for most of the book except for the last two chapters, which reveal some hesitation. As for the inserted chapters-to-be, the first first one referring to the "Cadre du baptême" became Chapter IV of the published novel. The next insert, a chapter of conspiracy and politics, was never added as such, but was merely incorporated into others. The final note containing an idea for a chapter on the elections of 1857 was also absorbed into another chapter.

Each of the above chapter outlines was then expanded in the worksheets. They are to be found inserted in somewhat haphazard order among the outlines for the initial chapter plan, an arrangement which makes it rather difficult to follow the sequences of composition. At any rate, Chapters I, II, and III[36] have one clear form which is identical with that of the novel as written. Chapter IV, the baptism, is the elaboration of the insert in the chapter outline. Then we have a chapter outline (*f.* 23) that mentions the baptism for the first time. The point of view for the description was to be through Rougon rather than Gilquin, although the latter is mentioned as seated at a café. The chapter would close with a view of an old barricade, an ironic commentary on the dark origins of this glorious regime. Zola then recomposed his outline (*ff.* 19-22) in a form identical with that of the final text of the novel.

At this point Zola started splitting his chapter outlines. First, he took the outline for the third chapter in the *first*

---

[36] Chapter i is the scene at the Chamber of Deputies where the money for the baptism is voted, and Rougon is about to fall from power. Chapter ii shows Rougon's clique, as he cleans up his office after his downfall. Chapter iii is Rougon's first visit to Clorinde's apartment.

plan ("Mon aventurière. Elle tente Rougon. Leurs amours.
Il la marie.") and commented: "Dans ce chapitre, je peux
en tailler plusieurs" (*f.* 32). He then elaborated Rougon's
visit to Clorinde's apartment, where her portrait is being
painted. His lust for her sweeps over him. Here we have
Chapter III of the novel. Then Zola allows for a chapter
for their "love affair": "Elle vient à cheval. La scène de la
serre; puis l'explication (poser largement Delestang) et le
mariage avec l'ami." It is not hard to see the evolution of
this basic idea into Rougon's attack in the stable in Chapter
V. Zola allows another chapter for "la vie de l'homme politique tombé." This outline anticipates the final form of Chapter VI. "Il est à la campagne. Les soirées. La conspiration
de tous ces gens pour le remettre au pouvoir . . . . Son ennui,
son bâillement de lion, lui qui a touché au pouvoir" (*ff.*
32-33). Chapter VII, the visit to Compiègne, is an isolated
section of the novel, and therefore clear enough in the author's
mind to necessitate but one outline (*ff.* 36-38, 40). In the
middle of *feuillet* 40, Zola begins what will be the next
chapter, the one in which Rougon despairs of ever coming to
power again, but the fortuitous attempt of Orsini to assas-
sinate the Emperor comes to his rescue (*ff.* 40-41). Then
these last two sheets were rewritten as a separate chapter
(*ff.* 42-45) and thus Chapter VIII was prepared. Each of
the remaining chapters in the novel (Chapters IX-XIV)
has a double outline: the first one is a bit general, and covers
sometimes the material for two chapters, but then is broken
down in detail and assumes exactly the form that one finds
in the published book.

This somewhat detailed examination of the composition
of the various chapters indicates that Zola's general method
for *Son Excellence Eugène Rougon* was no different from
that for many other volumes of the *Rougon-Macquart*. The

differences were ones of detail caused by the specific problems of the particular novel. One may note primarily that the chapters which show, according to the hope mentioned in the *ébauche,* "une large page sociale et humaine," the ones in which a large panorama is offered to the reader's view, i.e., the baptism and the weekend at Compiègne, were added late. This fact would seem to re-emphasize that Zola's basic desire was rather that which he had announced on the very first sheet of his notes: "Histoire d'un parti, d'une coterie, poussant son chef et le dévorant." Zola was more concerned with the mechanism of the rise and fall of his protagonist than with anything else. Except for these two above-mentioned spectacles, the historical details would be selected, and if necessary trimmed, to serve this basic purpose.

The Historical Sources

        *I*n organizing his novel, Zola had
to be careful with the chronology. On some occasions in
other works he was willing to alter the dates a little, but for
the key political events of a regime, he had to remain faithful
to history. We have already seen that in order to leave
room for a second political novel, he decided to end *Son Excellence Eugène Rougon* in 1860 or 1861 with the proclamation of the Liberal Empire. The novel would now begin,
not with the Marshal Pélissier episode, but with the voting
the credit for the baptism of the Imperial Prince. There were
only two other key dates. One was the election of June 1857,
which was to be but a minor part of the story and could be
made to fit in anywhere, but the other one was of capital importance. Orsini's attack upon the Emperor's life in January

1858, the consequent elevation of the strong-armed General Espinasse to the head of the Ministry of the Interior, and his fall from grace five months later, were the historical events that Zola used to create a situation in which his authoritarian might return to power. Around these dates, Zola built his novel. In order to avoid serious errors in chronology, he wrote the month and year by each chapter heading of his second chapter plan outline (f. 2).[1] For example, he arranged it quite neatly so that the visit to Compiègne would be in the fall, when the famous week-long parties of the Imperial couple were actually held. The final chapter (March 1861) is really an epilogue with two and one-half years separating it from the preceding chapter. Consequently, it did not need to be tied in so carefully from the standpoint of chronology.

But there was one part of the time-problem that must have caused Zola some trouble. Rougon falls at the moment when the funds for the baptism are voted, and since he does not regain power until January 1858 (after the Orsini attempt), he must mark time for well over a year and a half. Zola had planned for him step down for a short time only, and had the novel started in February 1857, the wait would have been less than a year. But when Zola changed the beginning of the novel so that it opened in early 1856, the chronology was thrown off. It is evident that in order to fill in the long months of waiting, Zola had to use all his ingenuity: the baptism itself, the loves and feuds of Rougon and Clorinde, the visit to Compiègne. These scenes are skilfully handled, but still the wait seems agonizingly long. This time factor helps perhaps to explain the rather strange Chapter VIII. At Compiègne Clorinde had badly shaken

[1] These dates not always followed exactly in the final form of the novel. Sometimes they are a month or so off.

Marsy's favor with the Emperor. By seducing Marsy, she so infuriated Mme de Llorentz, his mistress, that the outraged lady deposited on the Emperor's desk three letters in which Marsy had made fun of the Empire and of Napoleon III himself. One would expect the irate Emperor to ask Marsy to resign. But nothing happens. Months pass as Clorinde and Rougon wait helplessly. Why? Zola must wait until mid-January of the following year for Orsini to hurl his bombs, even though Rougon has already been waiting a long time in Chapter VI. Rather than suppress these few months, as he could easily have done, Zola turned the long wait to his advantage. In the midst of the inaction and waiting, tempers become frayed, the group around the former minister begins to despair, and Rougon the Magnificent must plead with his band of sordid nonentities to stay with him just a little bit longer.[2] He even has a premonition that something will break in his favor, and finally, of course, it does. But this period of anxious waiting has given us one of Zola's most unusual chapters. Normally there is more action in his writing.

There is only one other slight difficulty with the chronology, a minor matter of which today's reader might not even be aware.[3] Rougon's second fall from power is timed with that of General Espinasse, and it must come five months after his rise to power—that is, in June 1858. At this moment in the novel there is a huge charity sale in which all the court ladies play an active role. As it happens, most of the social festivities did not take place in the summer, when Tout-

<hr>

[2] Jouvenel, in his *Vie de Zola* (Paris, 1931), pp. 128-129, says that Rougon's *désœuvrement* corresponds to Zola's when writing *SEER*. This is possible, and Zola's correspondence does reveal a period of jittery idleness (letter of Aug. 14, 1875; *Correspondance*, p. 433), but there is no direct evidence linking it to the novel.

[3] Excluding certain anachronisms in the speeches of the final chapter. See below for full treatment (pp. 56-59).

Paris was preparing to leave for Baden-Baden or the Channel, but perhaps as if conscious of this slight inaccuracy, Zola does not mention the exact month. Despite such minor matters, however, *Son Excellence Eugène Rougon* is consistent with historical chronology, and the more that one examines the text, the more this fidelity to chronology becomes evident. This is equally true of the historical content of the novel, as we shall now see. The German critic Keins states that the novel is only Zola's attempt to justify his hatred of the Empire.[4] Investigation of the history of the period shows that Zola's attitude was largely merited.

Of the fourteen chapters of *Son Excellence Eugène Rougon*, only four are pure fiction,[5] the others being built around various political or social events of the Second Empire. But even in these four chapters which describe Rougon's squabbles with his little band of leeches, and his duel with the adventuress Clorinde, Zola has derived from historical persons of that era many details in the lives of his two principal characters. While it is now generally recognized that Zola's documentation for his novels was often superficial, by that genius that seemed to guide him even when he did not always have full knowledge of a subject, he composed a novel which was accurate in much of its detail, a novel that did not accept as true many scurrilous rumors of the day. This was a creditable achievement, when one considers how little he liked the regime of Napoleon III, and how hostile were even serious Republican historians of the late nineteenth century.

The purpose of the first chapter, describing a session at the *Corps législatif,* is to reveal the Assembly's servile ac-

[4] Jean-Paul Keins, "Des Historisches Wahrheitsgehalt in den Romanen Zolas," *Romanische Forschungen,* XLVI (1932), 373.
[5] Chaps. ii, iii, v, xii.

ceptance of whatever propositions the Emperor had to make.[6]
For the descriptive part of his chapter, Zola went, as was
his custom, to visit the locale, drew a floor-plan of the building, and took notes on the contents of the hall and the ante-
chambers (see *ff*. 209-234). As for the proceedings, Zola
used the account published in the *Moniteur Universel* of
May 15, 1856, reporting on the *séance* of May 13. The
scathing picture of the Empire and of its representatives
that is presented in the first chapter is almost entirely historical. First, the minutes of the previous session are read,[7]
then various requests for leave by certain members are announced.[8] Zola has changed only the names. Then, as the
deputies chatter unconcernedly about private matters, a committee on various bills of local interest reports its findings.
They are all about the same, a request by a department to bor-
row money, or a petition for two small communes to merge
administratively. One can easily understand why there were
scarcely one hundred deputies present for such boring routine
matters, and not one of these was listening. If to the modern
reader this procedure of having the central government make
minor decisions for the departments represents serious overcentralization of power, it merely conforms to the French
system.[9] While these specific cases are not those mentioned in

[6] In addition to his earlier plan of presenting the scene of the grant to
Marshal Pélissier, he had also toyed with the idea of starting with the day
that the *Corps législatif* had voted to permit the Chief of State to accord
by decree pensions of 20,000 fr. (max.) to widows and children of high
functionaries to a total of 500,000 per year. Hamel, I, 188; Zola's *f*. 173.

[7] Antoine Laporte, *Le Naturalisme ou l'Immoralité littéraire* (Paris,
1894), p. 222. Laporte, a violent anti-Zola critic of the era goes so far
as to say that of course no minutes of the previous session were read,
for that would take up the entire session. Such willful misinterpretations
were not uncommon.

[8] For the number of members comprising the legislature and the various governmental bodies, as for their salaries, Zola took the information
(*ff*. 177-178) from Hamel (I, 43-55).

[9] Hamel was worried about this overcentralization, as noted by Zola
on *f*. 188.

the report on the May 13th session (perhaps Zola merely
changed the names, or perhaps he took them from the account
of some other day's proceedings), they are entirely accurate
in spirit. Zola then gives us the highlight of the day's action:
the report on the credits for the baptism. Now all the deputies
arrive to take their seats, since each of these political lackeys
wishes to show his devotion to the Emperor by voting for
this bill. The text of this colorful report is presented verbatim in the novel (pp. 20-23) without a word changed.
Zola was apparently fascinated by the political oratory of the
day. One will remember that he had previously copied *in
toto* the speech in behalf of Marshal Pélissier. In both cases,
one finds the same balanced cadences, the noble words, all
the orotund oratory. The legislature hastened to vote in
favor, 239-0. Zola dutifully transcribed the tally in his novel.
However, the session is not yet over. After manifesting
their undying fidelity to the Emperor, many deputies leave
at once, for the Assembly returns immediately to the dull
rountine of laws of local interest. But before ending his
chapter, Zola wished to show the power of the executive
dominating the legislative body. For this incident he used
the session of June 30 of that year, reported in the July 2nd
issue of the *Moniteur*. The incident was trivial. The government planned to build a new courthouse in the department of
the Pyrénées Orientales at Perpignan, a building that would
cost some 150,000 francs, to be paid over a period of twelve
years.[10] It so happened, however, that the head of the legislative committee, a M. Justin Durand, felt that the expendi-
ture was not necessary and politely said so, even though he
was alone against the rest of the committee. But when it
became clear that the Minister of Finance was in favor

[10] Résumé of these items on Zola's *f*. 226; Zola's source, however, is
not indicated in his notes.

of the idea, he withdrew his objection and the bill was voted unanimously. Zola dramatized this routine incident to show that if someone was bold enough to oppose the government-sponsored bill, he was careful to use the most courteous language. Zola also wished to remind his reader that under Napoleon III, when a minister spoke, usually all obeyed at once. Hence this incident is entirely historical, except for one minor—yet significant—change. Not only did Zola exaggerate the fawning manner of the lone opponent, but he also made the protester a simple deputy, *not* a member of the committee, in order to emphasize the helpless subservience of the legislature. Artistically the change was a good one, and in truth, it was not unfair politically, since in 1856 the *Corps législatif* was a rubber stamp for the Emperor.

In his description that serves as a background for the action in the Assembly, Zola reminds us that the Reporters' Gallery has been missing since 1852, because there is no freedom of the press; the speaker's rostrum has likewise been suppressed, and the deputies must speak from their benches on the floor, a position in which they are, significantly, lower than under the Republic; finally, a curtain covers a fresco of Louis-Philippe swearing to uphold the charter. Would it remind the people that Napoleon III had once sworn to support the Constitution of the Second Republic? In short, action and setting combine to portray a useless, powerless legislature, bored with its own existence, and as the long afternoon draws to a close, the shadows drown the hall in darkness (p. 27). This picture may seem too hostile to some, and there is no denying that Zola emphasizes the passivity of the Chamber so that it may form a contrast with the tumultuous session of the final chapter. Nonetheless, the initial picture of the *Corps législatif* remains an essentially accurate one.

For the baptism of the young Imperial Prince, Zola had available a variety of sources, in Taxile Delord[11] as well as in Hamel,[12] not to mention the memoirs of the people who had witnessed the colorful spectacle. But the main source was, once again, the *Moniteur Universel* of June 15, 1856, which reported at great length the festivities of the fourteenth: the procession to Notre-Dame, the order of march, the position of the innumerable dignitaries. Zola took extensive notes from his sources (*ff.* 245-254) presumably from the *Moniteur* itself, for his notes follow the sequence of the official account, and he refers to the newspaper by name on *f.* 222.

The account in the official government newspaper is, in places, colorfully written.[13] Zola needed only to break it up, change a few words here and there, suppress long lists of the names of the dignitaries, and he had the core of his chapter. There remained the task of finding a focal object on which to center the description, for to the Republican and non-religious Zola, who refers at the end of the book (through a character) to the young Prince as "le crapaud" (p. 381), the baptism had no transcendental reality and no emotional appeal. He chose as the center of his description the Arcole bridge, with its glorious Napoleonic echoes. For the meaning of his chapter, he again prepared a contrast with a later chapter where, following the attempt on the Emperor's life, Paris would be painted all in black, a symbol of trouble. Here, all is blue, gold, and white, sunshine and serene happiness, indeed

[11] II, 10.
[12] II, 192-194.
[13] The style is not too unlike Zola's. E.g.:"Une foule immense qu'augmentaient encore, à chaque instant, des flots de voyageurs arrivés par les trains de plaisir, se pressait depuis le matin dans les rues. . ."

"l'apogée de l'empire." At the last minute[14] he added a final touch: painted on a building high above the procession to the cathedral, a man's overcoat can be seen. It is actually some bit of advertising, but by chance, the garment resembles the famous overcoat of Napoleon I. One of the characters points to it saying "Tiens, l'oncle là-bas" (p. 100), and the crowd laughs. The symbolism is not the less effective for being obvious: the Second Empire always claimed to place itself under the auspices of *Napoléon le grand*, but alas, Napoleon I was dead and his Empire as empty as the overcoat painted on the wall. *Napoléon le petit* displayed the pomp of parading military units; he received representatives from various courts of Europe, the Cardinal-Legate,[15] and former Napoleonic royalty.[16] But he could not re-create the glorious First Empire. His regime carried on no previous legitimate government and by implication had no legitimacy of its own.

In addition to this political criticism, Zola attacked the high cost of the baptism. The layette of the child cost in itself 100,000 francs; the procession alone came to 172,000 francs. The total cost was nearly 900,000 francs in one form or another.[17] The novelist was careful to retain these historical details (p. 90), although he failed to mention (because Hamel was careful not to mention) that some 200,000 francs

[14] It does not appear either in the *ébauche* or in any of the chapter plans.

[15] Napoleon III had asked the Pope to come, and was very disappointed to receive merely a representative. The Pontiff was, however, godfather to the child.

[16] The novel indicates (p. 98) that Jérôme Bonaparte was there. In this respect Zola follows the *Moniteur's* account, which had been released in advance. As it happened, Jérôme was sick and could not attend. The next day's newspaper carried a correction, but Zola did not see it.

[17] Hamel, II, 192. Hamel found this information in the papers seized at the Tuileries after the downfall of the Empire in 1870. *Papiers et correspondances de la famille impériale*, t. 1 (Paris: Imprimerie nationale, 1870), p. 80.

of the total sum was given as charity to various worthy organizations. But despite Zola's insistence on the Emperor's extravagance, he laid aside his satire and gave free rein to his descriptive powers. The result is a magnificent and not totally unsympathetic portrayal of this colorful event.

All was well for the Empire, or so it seemed. There were natural disasters, like the floods of 1856, that were carefully included in the novel (pp. 90,105),[18] but the country was prosperous, the Empire solidly supported by a majority of the French. When, however, it came time for the elections of 1857, the government not only designated its candidates, but also brought tremendous pressure to bear on their behalf and frightened most of the opposition into silence. One of the few voices raised in protest was that of our historian Ernest Hamel, who resolutely ran as a Republican. He ruefully tells of his experience:

> On tremblait de me voir, on avait peur de mon salut: plusieurs personnes, même celles qui m'étaient favorables, me firent prier de ne pas mettre les pieds chez elles, pour ne pas les compromettre. . . . Enumérerai-je les abus d'autorité, mes affiches lacérées, mes bulletins jetés par milliers dans les fossés? Un jour, à Péronne, on arrêta, sans autre forme de procès, un débitant de boissons qui avait bien voulu se charger de la distribution de mes circulaires (II, 229).

Zola paid his debt to Hamel by including his story—anonymously—in the novel (p. 143).

Zola had copied extensively[19] the mechanism by which the government "supported" its own candidates. Billault, the Minister of the Interior, sent out a circular in May 1857, which despite a firm tone, was not without fairness: "Au jour de l'élection, le vote sera secret et les scrutins seront dépouillés sous les yeux de tous. La vérité et l'indépendance

[18] Hamel, II, 192; Zola's *f*. 173.
[19] Hamel, II, 230; Zola's *f*. 174.

du suffrage sont donc garanties." He stated also that "les candidatures contraires pourront librement se produire." Billault must not have been satisfied with the moderate nature of these instructions, for on June 1 he sent another circular "très confidentielle." This one read that

chaque candidat pouvant librement faire afficher et distribuer ses circulaires et professions de foi, les réunions électorales n'auraient pas d'utilité réelle, et ne sauraient avoir pour but que d'exciter et d'agiter les esprits, vous ne les permettrez pas.

Vous ne tolérerez pas davantage les comités électoraux. Tous ces moyens artificiels de propagande n'ont d'autre résultat que de substituer l'influence de quelques meneurs au bon sens impartial des masses.[20]

It is no wonder then that Rougon says admiringly of the circulars[21] for the 1857 elections that this last one was "d'une jolie force" (p. 148).

These instructions were strong, but out of fear or desire for promotion, many local mayors and prefects interpreted them even more strongly. One such example was the Plassiart affair, although Zola did not use it directly.[22] Plassiart, who was a mayor and an official government candidate for the post of "conseiller général," used bribes and threats of all kinds. His son, director of the local post office, violated the secrecy of the mails; the two of them marked ballots, and when the mayor counted the result of the vote for his own election, he falsified flagrantly. In this case the pair were caught, tried, and convicted, but as the conservative Delord comments: How many, nearly as guilty, were not? The autocratic system produced such evils, and cases of invalidation of Republican ballots were common. Also widespread was the system of marking the ballots so that they were no

[20] Hamel, II, 227-228.
[21] In the novel they were sent out by Marsy (i.e. Morny) rather than by Billault.
[22] Referred to both by Delord, III, 91-92, and Hamel, III, t. 2, 252.

longer secret, with the result that many people became more cautious in their voting. Even so, five anti-Bonapartist Republican deputies were returned from Paris.[23] Zola copied this final detail, although without mentioning any names. While he might have added that several Legitimist and Orleanist deputies were returned from the Provinces, he was a fundamentally accurate historian.

Chapter VII is a return to gaiety with the court at Compiègne. Each fall, at the Imperial residence near Paris, various dignitaries, artists, and prominent members of society were invited for a week as guests of the Emperor and Empress. Because there was a series of these parties throughout the fall, they became known as *séries*. These festivities were certainly worth including in the novel, for by their gay but conservative brilliance, they well represented the high social life of the Court. Furthermore, Zola would be able to throw together various figures who normally moved in different spheres. For his documentation Zola turned to Paul Dhormoys' *La Cour à Compiègne, Confidences d'un valet de chambre*.[24] Actually Dhormoys was a journalist who gained access to Compiègne by pretending to be the manservant accompanying an artist friend of his. The book is no exposé. Quite the contrary, it paints nearly everything in decorous and complimentary terms. Zola did well to use such a conservative document because the most scurrilous tales were circulated about what went on there: e.g. that the Emperor would toss a handful of jewels on the floor and leer at the exposed legs of the ladies who were scrambling around on all fours for the gems. Perhaps it was Flaubert, who had been at Compiègne, who reassured his friend that all was quite proper—even dull—at these *séries* (except for the

[23] Hamel, II, 234.
[24] Paris, 1866. Previously published in instalment form in 1865 in *L'Evénement.*

Emperor's nocturnal escapades). At any rate, Zola followed Dhormoys' account nearly word for word. The journalist indeed painted a fascinating picture: The distinguished guests arrived in considerable confusion, quarreled over who get the "best" rooms, finally changed dress, and awaited the arrival of the Imperial couple in La Galerie des Cartes. When their majesties arrived, Napoleon passed down the ranks of the visitors and greeted everyone, especially those who were his guests for the first time. An elegant and tasteful dinner was then served for nearly one hundred persons. After coffee in the Galerie, there was dancing and the Emperor often played a form of shuffleboard (*palets*). Sometimes there were charades and *tableaux vivants,* that rage of the period, satirized by Zola in *La Curée.* The program for the next day, Dhormoys tells us, included a deer hunt and a visit by several chosen guests to the Empress' tea in her *petits appartements,* where elegance and wit were the order of the day. On the evening after the hunt, by the light of many torches, there occurred the celebrated *curée froide.* The unleashed hunting dogs, at first restrained by visual signal alone, were finally allowed to hurl themselves onto the still-warm entrails of the deer.

Zola followed all these events with great care, and even placed them in the same sequence with occasional simplifications. For example, there is only one deer, not two, in the novel, and there is no delay due to bad weather, etc.[25] In general, however, Zola kept even the slightest details: place names, a certain mechanical piano, the Emperor's dog Nero,[26]

[25] The last half of Dhormoys' book describes a bird-shooting expedition, with incredible numbers of birds killed. Apparently Zola did not use it because he had ample material without it.

[26] The scene in the novel (p. 179) that shows a high-ranking official slobbering over the dog is to be found in Dhormoys (p. 42). Zola omitted to state, however, that the man was the former owner of the animal. The impression that the reader receives is that the court official tended toward utter senility. The omission was hardly fair.

the brief, noisy appearance of the Imperial Prince, the cost
of wood for the many fireplaces (estimated at 1500 francs
per day), and so forth. There are of course some changes
from Dhormoys' account, for Zola writing as a novelist had
to weave his plot into the festivities. Consequently, Clorinde
is there seducing Marsy, Rougon is agitating for a program to establish experimental farms and agricultural co-
operatives. There are other changes as well. The dinner-
table conversation, not mentioned by Dhormoys, in the novel
becomes quite ribald at times, and an aura of seduction and
sensuality pervades the dining hall.[27] Zola was only filling
in an omission in Dhormoys' book, published with official
approval. Napoleon III, whose weakness for women was
well known, passed up no opportunities to acquire a new
mistress. He prowled around the dancers and groups of
chattering guests, carefully watched in turn by various wom-
en trying to gain his favor.[28] If the gentlemen were often
ribald, they were largely inspired by the low-cut gowns of
the ladies. Nevertheless, for many sophisticates, the evenings
were impossibly dull because the Empress forbade certain
daring games. Zola echoes this view by presenting a novelist there who decides that it is *crevant* (p. 176). Even so,
most of the guests were delighted to be present, especially
the women, who had an excuse for buying expensive new
clothes.[29] Indeed, they must have found the *curée froide*
worth the cost of the entire visit. Zola makes only two

[27] An indelicate observation was omitted from the *feuilleton* version.
Speaking of a low-cut gown, a man says: "Il y en a un qui va sortir,
pour sûr. Hein? celui de gauche" (p. 171).
[28] E.g., Mme de Taisey-Chatenoy (pseud. for Marquise Irène de Gengoux) *A la cour de Napoléon III* (Paris, 1891), recounts how she was
made Queen for a Night. Even allowing for exaggeration, one must
conclude that the Emperor lacked discretion.
[29] In his plan for this chapter, Zola quotes Dhormoys (p. 11) who
is passing on a *mot* of that era: "Je suis invité à Compiègne, j'ai vendu
un moulin."

changes in Dhormoys' account of it. The first is the big
dog that bursts into the pack to rip out his part of the entrails. To all appearances, the incident symbolizes Rougon's
coming return to power. The other change is the reaction of
the onlookers, particularly the women, who quiver in animal
excitement at the scene. Zola never lets one forget how
close we all are to *la bête humaine.*

In Chapter VIII we revert to politics. Zola chose the
Orsini affair as the historical event through which Rougon
regains his political power. Félix Orsini and his three accom-
plices hurled bombs at the Emperor's carriage in front of
the Opéra on January 14, 1858. True to history, although
not mentioning the names of the plotters, Zola recounts the
event very briefly (p. 227), mentioning the Emperor's
miraculous escape and the number of casualties among the
innocent bystanders. As for the perpetrators of the attack,
Zola writes (p. 220) that there were four Italians: an elderly
man of about fifty years of age, small, thin and sickly; another a young man of twenty-five. Of the other two, one
is mentioned as being young, whereas the last one is presented
in greater detail: "d'un âge mur, très beau, avec une face
pâle, de longs cheveux noirs, qui semblait être le chef." These
are accurate descriptions of the four plotters: Joseph Piéri,
Charles de Rudio, Antoine Gomez, and of course Félix
Orsini.[30]

The consequences of Orsini's crime, despite the fact that
no Frenchman participated in it,[31] were many. Napoleon
III asked General Espinasse to assume the post of Minister
of the Interior on February 7, 1858. No sooner had the

[30] Hamel's account of the Orsini affair is referred to on Zola's *f.* 175.
We have followed Hamel in gallicizing the first names.

[31] A detail emphasized by Zola, p. 233, taken from Hamel, II, 263.
I am indebted to E.M. Grant, *op. cit.,* for the material on Zola's use
of the repressions that followed the Orsini attempt.

general entered into his functions than he sent out a circular addressed to all French prefects stating that now "c'est aux bons à se rassurer et aux méchants seuls à trembler."[32] But even if Espinasse was temperamentally suited for his job, it was the Emperor himself who wrote him on February 15:

Le corps social est rongé par une vermine dont il faut, coûte que coûte, se débarrasser, malgré leurs protecteurs. Je compte pour cela sur votre zèle. *Ne cherchez pas, par une modération hors de saison,* à rassurer ceux qui vous ont vu venir au ministère avec effroi.   Il faut qu'on vous craigne. . . .[33]

In order to implement the Emperor's decree, the legislature passed, with only minor opposition, the *loi de sûreté générale,* which provided that anyone who had even been a troublemaker[34] might be deported to Algeria, or even beyond —to Cayenne or Lambessa. Zola was quick to note the fact that 380 deportees had already left by mid-March and that a convoy was leaving Toulon every week.[35]   In order to "pacify" the country, Espinasse had a list prepared of all the departments, with an arbitrary number of arrests to be made in each.   The prefects came to Paris and were told to arrest a given number. When one of them was naïve enough to ask for the names of those who should be arrested, he was told that this minor matter was up to him. This incredible tale is told by Hamel[36] but it is even more likely that Zola took it from Taxile Delord,[37] where the account is more dramatic, more detailed, and corresponds more closely to Zola's, even as to the wording (p. 258).

[32] Hamel, II, 264. Zola quotes it in novel on p. 233.
[33] *Ibid.*
[34] Article 2. Cited by Hamel, II, 264. Zola's novel, p. 233.
[35] Zola fails to mention that most deportees were amnestied within a year. In the novelist's favor, one should hasten to add that the amnesty hardly justified the deportations.
[36] II, 271 *et seq.*; Zola's *f.* 176.
[37] II, 385.

Zola gives one example of the workings of this barbarous law, the death of a M. Lebrun[38] in the department of Cher, and manages to work this historical account into part of his story. In the novel, Lebrun is a M. Martineau, who is accused, probably falsely, by an avaricious sister eager to lay hands upon his property.[39] This tragic scene takes place, not in Cher, but in Deux-Sèvres at the time of Rougon's political visit. The unsavory Gilquin plays the role of the police officer in charge who brings about Martineau's death in his hurry to return to a dance. Once again Zola's source might be Hamel (II, 273), where the tale is told briefly but completely. Hamel himself undoubtedly read it in E. Ténot and A. Dubost *Les Suspects de 1858* (Paris, 1869), and it is of course possible that Zola also read it there[40] (although this work is not mentioned in the worksheets) for the details check in many small ways. Here is their historical account:

En entrant, le brigadier Lafond annonce au citoyen Lebrun qu'il a un mandat d'amener contre lui. "Je suis prêt à vous suivre, répond celui-ci, mais puis-je savoir ce qu'on me reproche?

—Je n'ai pas mission de vous en instruire, répond le brigadier. —Nous avons aussi un mandat de perquisition, ajoute le commissaire de police Réthel.

—Libre à vous, dit Lebrun, rien ici n'est secret. Voilà la clef de mon bureau.

—Nous allons commencer à faire une perquisition sur votre personne," ajoute le brigadier et en disant cela, il se jette sur le citoyen Lebrun, saisit de sa main gauche les deux pans de

[38] The reason for his arrest, according to Hamel (II, 273) was that he was a cousin of the outspoken socialist, Michel de Bourges.

[39] One of the accusations, that Martineau had said, "Je me moque de l'Empereur" (p. 270), is actually from Hamel, II, 260: "Je me moque bien du *Te Deum* de l'Empereur." A relative of Hamel, a factory owner, was denounced by a worker for having uttered the phrase. The owner spent three months in prison for his comment.

[40] Noted by E.M. Grant, "Studies on Zola's *SEER*," p. 27.

son gilet et plonge la main droite dans les poches de son paletot. Il retire quelques papiers insignifiants . . . . Alors il secoue violemment le citoyen Lebrun, le presse contre sa poitrine avec une révoltante brutalité.

A ce moment, le citoyen Lebrun s'affaisse sur lui-même et tombe sur le parquet : il était paralysé de tout le côté droit, bras et jambe droits refusant tout service . . . . La famille voulut envoyer immédiatement chercher un médecin. Le gendarme, non encore satisfait, le défendait en disant "qu'il avait ordre de ne laisser sortir personne." Cependant, le domestique, prenant une autre issue, fut en quérir un qui arriva quelques instants après . . . .

Then a second doctor arrives, and the two of them, who are tout tremblants devant le terrible brigadier qui prétend que la paralysie est feinte, disent cependant que Lebrun ne peut être transporté dans cet état. "Si, répondent en chœur les quatre représentants de l'autorité, nous l'emmenons," et, comme la voiture s'attelait lentement, le brigadier ajouta : "Si dans cinq minutes il n'est pas dans la voiture, je l'attache sur la croupe de mon cheval et ce ne sera pas long."

Mme Lebrun voulut monter dans la voiture à côté de son mari. "Point de ça," dit le commissaire. "Voilà une autre voiture, montez-y ; mais quant à lui, il restera seul." Il fallut obéir. (pp. 216-219)

One can readily see the similarity, even in the smallest details to Zola's account in the novel, which includes the policeman's bodily attack upon the innocent citizen, the claim that the paralysis is faked, the slowness of the carriage to appear, and the exclusion of the wife from the carriage. The final scene of this tragedy is also true to history. At the prison the officials hestitate to receive a man in such condition, and he is therefore taken to a nearby hotel, where he dies. Zola legitimately made the most of the pathetic story as he closed the chapter with savage satire, giving the reader a vision of the happy carefree couples dancing at the Prefecture, celebrating Rougon's arrival in town.

This visit to Deux-Sèvres by Rougon concerns a railroad concession that Kahn finally obtains without paying the million franc bribe that Marsy is trying to extort from him. Kahn wants the tracks to make an unnecessary turn by some blast furnaces that he owns and which are on the verge of bankruptcy. The advantage of a nearby railroad would save him—at public expense. Rougon has exerted his influence as Minister to have the concession granted to Kahn, and has now come to celebrate the beginning of the construction. By this maneuver, he is also able to support Du Poizat, prefect of Deux-Sèvres. Is all this historical? Yes, but it is a composite picture. First, Eugène Rouher, after whom Rougon, as we shall see later on, is largely patterned, made a trip to Corrèze in 1863 for precisely the purpose of supporting an official candidate in danger of political defeat. Rougon in fiction and Rouher in history used the classic devices of the carrot and the stick, reminding the people that if they vote for the Emperor, public funds will be expended in their area, resulting in a veritable paradise for all.

As to the railroad affair, Zola was once more on solid ground. In his *notes particulières* (*ff.* 173-174), he transcribed from Hamel the affair of the Grand Central Railroad: "Morny avait fait obtenir des avantages à MM. de Pourtalès et de Ser [aincourt] pour une ligne de Clermont à Montauban, desservant les mines de ces messieurs."[41] The stock of the company controlling this stretch of track was quoted at eighty francs on the Bourse even before construction of the roadbed had begun, purely because it was known that Morny was in on it. But then Zola decided that the Belmontet affair was preferable.[42] This sordid tale dated from 1855. The Minister of Public Works had ordered that the

[41] Hamel, II, 219-220.
[42] *Ibid.*, II, 220; Zola's *f.* 173.

concession for the construction of a railroad from Bourges to
Montluçon, formally promised to the group that the *député*
Belmontet represented, a group openly backed by the Roths-
childs, be given to someone else. Then a representative of
Morny's came to tell Belmontet that for a million francs
worth of shares, Morny would be delighted to intercede in
their behalf. Belmontet refused this deal in righteous in-
dignation and wrote a letter to the Emperor, who apparently
did nothing about it.

Zola combined the two stories into one unsavory whole.
Rougon obtains a concession for Kahn to build his railroad;
then the shares are quoted at eighty francs (pp. 339-340)
before the work has even started. On top of this situation,
Zola superimposes the story of Marsy's (i.e., Morny's) attempted blackmail. One should add, in order to put this
swindle into perspective, that it was during this time that
the Second Empire did all it could to expand the French
railroad system in a hurry, for basic changes in the trans-
portation network of the country were necessary to help
France become a modern industrial nation. Therefore it
should come as no surprise that unscrupulous men were able
to take advantage of this rapid expansion.

In Chapter XI, there is more history, centered on one
of the Emperor's biweekly cabinet meetings at Saint-Cloud.
Its purpose in the development of the novel is to set Delestang, Clorinde's mediocre husband, against Rougon and to
pave the way for the latter's downfall. As Zola had no
friends who had been in the cabinet, and as Hamel and
Delord are understandably silent on the details of these closed
meetings, the novelist combined fact and fiction. In the novel
the ministers begin with an informal discussion of an acci-
dent suffered by some Paris dancer, and even the Emperor
himself seems *au courant* and solicitous of the lady's wel-

fare.[43]   However, the group reluctantly gets down to the business at hand. The main topic of conversation concerns new titles of nobility. Under the Empire a law was passed providing severe punishment for illegal usurpation of a noble title.[44] But the Emperor wished to go further, and authorized Persigny to draw up a whole new system of a nobility based on function. Hamel quotes at great length from the detailed proposal which suggests that after a given number of years of service, mayor and bishops will be made barons, and various higher dignitaries will be made counts.[45] Hamel concluded that only the disaster at Sedan kept the Emperor from trying to put this nonsense into effect.[46] As this idea was not submitted to the legislature, what would be more likely than to have it discussed at a private cabinet meeting where it would encounter enough opposition to make the Emperor decide to temporize? Zola followed Hamel closely, quoting verbatim the entire secton. He then shows the Emperor's approval of the plan, and the opposition that it encounters from Rougon and from members of the real nobility. Having ridiculed the Emperor for his pretty plan, Zola had but to turn the page of Hamel to find the Ministers' next topic of debate: censorship of *livres de colportage*,[47] those books or pamphlets that were hawked from village to village by itinerant peddlers. Throughout the nineteenth century many propaganda pamphlets were distributed in this way. Therefore it was only natural for Napoleon III to try to censor Socialist or Republican tracts by requiring

[43] A dramatic example of Zola's original pledge to expose how "se brassent les affaires dites sérieuses."

[44] May 1858, the month that this chapter takes place. The law is alluded to as having just been passed.

[45] II, 289.

[46] Not mentioned by Delord. Hamel claims to have the document with him as he writes.

[47] II, 291.

a seal of approval. A regulative commission was established in 1852.

Zola had already shown Rougon at work as a censor when he assumed power after Orsini's attack on Napoleon III. Rougon sends a warning to *Le Siècle* (p. 305) and storms at a newspaper editor because in a serialized novel a woman *bien élevée* deceives her husband and shows no remorse[48] (pp. 236, 261). Here at the cabinet meeting, it is a question of a book entitled *Les Veillées du bonhomme Jacques,* which, in dialogue form, preached in favor of agricultural co-operatives, extinction of pauperism, etc. While the majority of small propaganda leaflets was addressed to industrial workers, the more conservative farmers also received their share: it seems probable that Zola had seen such a pamphlet, and perhaps had done nothing but change its name slightly.[49]   Hamel does not refer to any such tract on economics, for his preoccupation is almost entirely political.   Delord is equally silent.   Hamel does, however, cite General Espinasse's harsh directives urging that no revolutionary propaganda be circulated.   In this, Zola follows history, having Rougon—here a re-creation of Espinasse—utilize the latter's order of June 14, 1858.   Then the novelist puts him in conflict with the Emperor's economic

[48] A curious coincidence: *Madame Bovary* was published as a *feuilleton* in the *Revue de Paris* from October to December 1856. At the famous trial, one of the main points of the prosecution was that this woman felt no remorse. The year does not quite coincide with that of the novel, but if Zola did not intend to refer to Flaubert's novel, he nonetheless succeeded in reminding the reader of it.

[49] Zola has no notes taken from any such tract, nor have we been able to locate any direct source. Prof. Guy Robert in his *La Terre d'Emile Zola: Étude historique et critique* (Paris, 1952), p. 195, refers to it, but gives no source either. The title might be a composite one, for many such pamphlets were entitled *Veillées* and the Bonhomme Jacques is reminiscent of the fourteenth century leader of *la jacquerie*. Robert notes that in 1885 there was published a title: *Les Veillées de Jacques Bonhomme.* It can only be a curious coincidence.

liberalism. The resulting clash of views provides an effective scene in the novel. Napoleon finds himself in disagreement with his minister, who can see only the Red Menace lurking behind this rather vapid propaganda tract. At this critical point Delestang, with his hazy economic utopianism, speaks out against Rougon and in so doing gains favor and prepares his future rise to power. Hence the chapter, while fictional, utilizes the history of the period to advance the story.[50]

Rougon's position has been shaken; in Chapter XIII he will fall from power. The incident that precipitates his downfall would give the average reader the impression that here, at least, the naturalist was giving free rein to his imagination. The story of the elderly couple battling with a religious order for an inheritance which they had never done anything to deserve is a cynically amusing one. The fierce greed of the Charbonnels seeking the five hundred thousand francs is rivaled by that of the religious order, which steals silver from the estate of the testator once the legal battle has been lost, thanks to Rougon's influence. And indeed, as far as anyone can tell, the episode is fictional; yet it also rings true historically. General Espinasse fell from power five months after he had assumed it, precisely for having attacked the clergy too vigorously. The Emperor was constantly irritating the Church by supporting Italian nationalism, but as he was forced to rely on clerical support, he found himself having to placate the prelates after incensing them. In this instance, Espinasse wished to force religious orders having lands yielding $2\frac{1}{2}$ to 3 per cent interest to sell the land and put the money into the fluctuating government *rentes,* which did in truth yield a better return. But

---

[50] Zola's following of the order of Hamel's book for the contents of this chapter would indicate that Lote's comment, *op. cit.,* p. 81, that Zola followed Delord even for the structure of the novel is incorrect.

the Church groups, preferring the lower yield and the greater
security of the land-based income, brought pressure to bear
on the Emperor for Espinasse's removal.

It was only a few years later that the government fought
the powerful Société de Saint-Vincent de Paul. In October,
1861, Persigny, then Minister of the Interior, decided that
all charitable organizations should be co-ordinated under one
government director. As the clerical group did not trust the
government, M. Ségur d'Aguesseau went so far as to suggest
in the Legislature that "l'auteur de ce circulaire pourrait
bien être traduit devant la haute cour."[51] Zola makes one
of his characters talk in nearly the same way over the Char-
bonnel incident, when Rougon orders the convent searched
for stolen silverware (pp. 348-349). As unrealistic as
Rougon's decision may seem to the modern American
reader, there actually were during the Second Empire some
cases of government search of a convent. They concerned not
silverware, but girls of Jewish parentage, who were being
converted to Christianity by overzealous prelates who hid
the girls away so that their parents could not find them. In
1861 there were two trials of such clerics.[52] While it would
be too much to say that Zola had all this in mind when he
wrote the novel, the impression that the reader receives is
a true one: the alliance between the Church and the State
was at best an uneasy one, and often had its sordid aspects.
It should be pointed out that in this case Rougon's actions
are far more unscrupulous than those of his adversary, the
Bishop. Rougon literally cheats the Fathers out of a perfectly legitimate inheritance. Here, at least, one cannot accuse the naturalist of excessive hostility to the Church.

The episode of Rougon's fall from power as a result of
his fight with the clergy and of Clorinde's efforts is a color-

[51] Delord, III, 242.   [52] *Ibid.,* III, 212 and 222.

ful one. The scene takes place in June 1858, which was also the time of Espinasse's fall, when the court was at Fontaine-bleau. Rougon, like the general, had sent in a resignation intended to reinforce his position with the confident hope that it would be rejected, for had not the Emperor constantly assured him of his support? Clorinde, however, has just seduced the Emperor and become his mistress. Her price is Rougon's dismissal and the elevation of her husband to power. This is the "canaillerie énorme" that Zola mentioned in the *ébauche*. The setting is a charity sale which Zola situates at the Orangerie des Tuileries.[53] Here the court ladies have set up booths and are selling various knick-knacks at high prices, with the profits going to charity. Zola's picture of it, however, is far from flattering. He writes: "la charité restait le prétexte" (p. 358), but real reason for the whole affair was to provide an occasion where the ladies might display themselves in low-cut gowns and vie with each other in attempting to seduce the masculine customers into buying cheap articles at very high prices. Zola used every possible device to emphasize the animality of the scene, and while Clorinde impudently displays a choker that reads "J'appartiens à mon maître," Mme de Combelot, who will be the Emperor's next favorite, so intoxicates the males that she manages to sell everything at her booth, the last article being a broken toothpick that goes for 117 francs![54]

Is this picture of the social life of the Second Empire, with its total absence of decent values, absurdly exaggerated? Two quotations are of interest. Ferdinand Bac, referring to another matter, writes:

la gaieté était trop franche, la maison de trop bon ton pour tourner à 'l'orgie de charité,' cette institution frelatée qui, sous

[53] Zola's *f*. 81 indicates that he had first planned it for the "serre du L." The Louvre? There was one at the time.
[54] In francs of 1858!

le couvert de Bonnes-œuvres, permet aux femmes de la meilleure souche de jouer des dénudées de music-hall. Personne de nos jours ne comprendrait rien au scandale que souleva la Comtesse de Castiglione.[55] Qu'on y songe: cette créature impudique avait osé montrer un décolleté téméraire dans des gazes de soie.[56]

And a second source confirms that such charity orgies were only too real. *La Vie Parisienne* of 1868 contains a skit showing worthy ladies trying to think of a new idea for "charity." And in the issue of March 7 of that year, one may read following account of the climax of one such sale:

Toutes ses marchandises épuisées, la jolie Madgyare fut pressée de vendre, pièce à pièce, les innombrables colifichets qui la couvraient. Quand je partis, les enchères s'entre-croisaient; le moindre clou était coté deux Napoléons [40 francs], on hâchait même ses rubans; jamais reliques n'inspiraient plus de piété. L'objet de ce délire se dépouillait avec une générosité qui eût dû être sans limites.

"Dame!," says the reporter, "Pour les pauvres!" The sarcasm is only too evident.

The final chapter leaves such amiable frivolities and we plunge once again into the purely political. The scene is the *Corps législatif* in 1861. On November 24 of the previous year, Napoleon III had issued a decree proclaiming the right of the legislature to issue an annual *adresse* to the Emperor and thus restored a privilege abolished in 1852. This measure was intended to introduce the Liberal Empire, for in this *adresse,* the legislature could, if it wished, discuss and criticize the government's general policy. Georges Lote has already mentioned the composite nature of this chapter, and E.M. Grant has amplified and corrected this initial work. In our turn, we shall draw heavily on what has already been ac-

---

[55] Already identified as the model for Clorinde Balbi. Cf. E.M. Grant, *op. cit.;* for full treatment, see chap. iv.
[56] *La Cour des Tuileries* (Paris, 1930), p. 54.

complished by these scholars. The chapter opens with the debate of the *adresse,* on March 14, 1861. An amendment, seeking increased civil liberties, has been submitted by the five Republican deputies (Favre, Darimon, Picard, Hénon, and Ollivier in actual history), but orderly discussion becomes impossible, so great is the tumult. The members of the Legislature are calling for order, and the President—the Count de Marsy—asks the unnamed speaker to repeat what he has said. The orator, obviously a Republican, says "J'ai dit que le deux décembre était un crime" (p. 389). The uproar becomes even greater. On this particular day, as E.M. Grant has pointed out, it was Jules Favre who made a firm speech in favor of this amendment, but nowhere is there any inflammatory sentence about the crime of December 2. This detail is not, as E.M. Grant perhaps implied, the product of Zola's vivid imagination. Late in March 1865, we read in Hamel that when the Chamber was discussing the *adresse*:

"Ne me parlez pas du deux décembre," lui cria M. Ernest Picard. M. Rouher protesta vivement. "Justifiez le deux décembre au point de vue de la loi," lui dit très parlementairement M. Jules Favre.

Alors M. Rouher: "Nous avons détruit les factions ce jour-là et nous les détruirions encore". . . .

Comme M. Jules Favre le mettait au défi d'oser dire qu'il agirait à l'égard de cette chambre, comme on avait agi avec l'Assemblée nationale, M. Picard laissa échapper cette parole vengeresse: "Le deux décembre est un crime."

Ces mots, que se garda bien d'enregistrer le journal officiel et qu'au milieu du bruit une partie seulement des membres du Corps législatif purent entendre, soulevèrent un formidable orage.

"A l'ordre! A l'ordre! cria-t-on de toutes parts."[57]

The source of Zola's incident is then clear, although there

[57] III, 217.

is no mention of it in his notes. Is it historically accurate?
It is difficult to say. The *Grand dictionnaire universel* of
Pierre Larousse tells the same story in its treatment of
Picard. There seems little reason to doubt it. The criminality
of the *coup d'état* had often been suggested by the Republican
opposition. It was only logical that it should finally be stated.
By using this highly colorful incident from another year,
Zola was able to give particular drama to his chapter.

Georges Lote suggested that as Rougon is a reflection
of Eugène Rouher, the latter's activities in 1867, when he
turned from a policy of authoritarianism to one of liberalism,
are the orgin of Rougon's activities in the last chapter of the
novel. But as E.M. Grant has shown,[58] his remarks are
almost identical with some statements of Pierre-Jules Baroche, one of the government's ministers without portfolio.
As an example, Hamel's summary of Baroche's words is
revealing:

Que venait-on parler de l'asservissement de la presse? Est-ce
que jamais une grande question, un intérêt sérieux avaient manqué d'organe parmi les journaux? La presse était, en effet, dans
les mains du gouvernement; le ministre voulut bien l'avouer.
Mais cela ne valait-il pas mieux que si elle était dans la main
de ses ennemis? Cet argument . . . obtint la vive approbation de
la majorité, dont il excita le rire prolongé.[59]

Rougon's speech is certainly based on it: "Si le gouvernement l'a prise [la presse] dans ses mains, c'est uniquement
pour ne pas la laisser aux mains de ses ennemis." And Zola
adds: "Des rires approbateurs s'élevèrent" (p. 398).

Rougon utters words of warning against the Red Menace and Rouher did likewise on more than one occasion, but
it was, curiously enough, the Republican Jules Favre, who
said on March 14, 1861, that "il avait combattu le drapeau

[58] P. 36.
[59] III, 25.

rouge, dans les plis duquel il lisait les mots detestés de despotisme et de servitude dont il ne voulait pas, qu'ils vinssent de la rue ou du trône."[60]

There is more. In this final chapter, Rougon makes two lengthy speeches which have the effect of dividing the chapter. It is in the second part that Rougon indicates the extent of his change of policy. The former anticlerical has to answer a statement favoring the maintenance of the Pope's temporal power. The orator's speech from the floor closes with "Il me déplaît que Venise la superbe, la reine de l'Adriatique, soit devenue l'obscure vassale de Turin."[61] Again in Hamel we read a report of session of March 11, 1861. M. Kolb-Bernard spoke as follows, according to the historian: "Il lui répugnait de voir 'Venise la superbe, la reine de l'Adriatique, devenue l'obscure vassale de Turin.' "[62] Hamel's caustic comment—"Il aimait mieux sans doute la voir dans les serres de l'Autriche"—is not transcribed by the novelist.

We have seen, then, that there is no doubt that Zola rearranged the historical speeches. But as E.M. Grant remarks, "he did not in all probability destroy verisimilitude by doing that."[63] The situation of voting the *adresse* is there, the clerical question was raised during that year.[64] Concerning Rougon's change from an authoritarian to a liberal viewpoint, as Lote has remarked, it does rather resemble Rouher's shift in attitude of 1867. We shall analyze the composition of Rougon as a character presently, but as for the basic history of the final chapter, it should not disturb any but the most punctilious historian. Such is not quite the case for the

[60] *Ibid.*; cited in *Moniteur* of March 15, 1861; E.M. Grant, p. 37.
[61] Turin was the center of Italian nationalism.
[62] II, 23.
[63] P. 38.
[64] An amendment to support the Pope's temporal power was offered in 1861 and received nearly 100 votes. E.M. Grant, p. 37.

whole novel. Without a doubt, the historical incidents were largely accurate in themselves, but were selected, rearranged, and used to a considerable extent for polemical and satirical purposes. But in the last analysis, Zola's history transcends the polemical, and in the best tradition of the historical novelist, he provides the reader with a highly colorful and genuinely informative tableau of the political mores of the regime of Napoleon III.

[Chapter Four]

The Characters

$\mathscr{W}$e have already seen that the plot of the novel is based on many historical incidents. In like fashion, several of the characters that move through the book can be shown to have historical prototypes. Of course, Napoleon III and the Empress are mentioned by name, although the latter appears only as a silhouette. We see her shortly before the birth of her son spending afternoons "à la création d'une maison d'éducation pour les jeunes filles pauvres" (p. 91), and once the child is born,[1] she refuses the gift of a large sum and turns the money over to an Orphan Training Center. These details are historically accurate, as

---

[1] A character says that "elle a eu des couches superbes" (p. 90). This is not entirely true. Complications kept her from having any more children. But it is not the author, only an uninformed and enthusiastic character who reports this item.

are the little receptions that she holds at Compiègne, which we have already mentioned.   It is interesting that Zola did not make any attempt to satirize her clerical views and pro-Vatican policy, and presented her rather sympathetically.

As to the Emperor himself, he appears in the novel in somewhat more complete fashion.   For his documentation, Zola turned to Flaubert, who could imitate Napoleon's gesture of twirling his waxed moustaches while he walked with a hesitant, slightly dragging step.[2]   There are also, of course, many allusions to the Emperor's personality and traits in Delord and Hamel, and Dhormoys' book was valuable for the chapter at Compiègne.   But in the last analysis, a person as important as Napoleon III was known to all; his caricature had appeared everywhere.   Consequently, Zola's picture resembles the Napoleon of the late Empire, a man already suffering from his malady.[3]   In the novel (pp. 301-302) he is portrayed as being "souffrant" at the cabinet meeting, his eye vacant and his whole person weary in the extreme.   During the period 1856-58 he had more energy.   Except for this slight error in timing, Zola's portrait of him is largely correct.   If he is pictured as an old lecher kissing Clorinde's feet with his moustache (p. 362), he is also shown as considerate and thoughtful, as when he inquires after the health of his guests at Compiègne (pp. 167-168).   Sometimes his personal considerateness was not a virtue, for he disbursed large sums of the state's money to his friends (p. 183).   All these facets of the man's personality—even though sketched briefly—are easily recognizable as based on fact.   The equally accurate portrayal of his economic liberalism and the indecisiveness of his foreign policy will be examined in detail in the next chapter.   At any rate, despite the political nature

[2] LeBlond, p. 408, citing the *Journal des Goncourt,* March 7, 1875.
[3] Dhormoys described him in 1865, at which time he was sometimes ill.

of the novel, the Emperor remained in the background, for to Zola his position was a static one. In trying to show the mechanism of the rise and fall of Rougon and of the other office-seekers, Zola emphasized continually the dynamic quality of the governmental structure. In such a portrayal, there was little need for the Emperor except as a presence or a force which might cause the others to get— or not to get—what they wanted.

Among the fictional characters three minor ones are traceable to certain personages of that era. For example, Beulin d'Orchère, the magistrate whose sister Rougon marries, is mentioned (p. 109) as having approved the decree for the spoliation of the Orléans family wealth.[4] He is also mentioned (p. 105) as President of the Court of Appeals. A reader familiar with the details of history would probably think of the Magistrate Troplong who held this same post and played an influential role in the attack on the Orléans family. As to Beulin d'Orchère's character, Zola constantly refers to him as "le dogue . . . . avec son lourd museau" (p. 106), and later, Clorinde suggests that he is about to start barking (p. 163). Here the trait seems to be borrowed from another magistrate—Delangle—who had also been active in the Orléans affair and became in 1853 "premier président de la cour de Paris." In Zola's novel Beulin d'Orchère rises to that very post (p. 239). As to the bulldog's face, it was apparently a noteworthy feature of Delangle, for many historians and memorialists refer to it. That Zola actually composed a composite minor character is hard to prove, although it seems probable; in any event, he succeeded in creating a representative magistrate of the era, competent, austere, but quick to use any means in order to advance himself professionally.

[4] Brief notes from Hamel (t. 2, I, 40) in Zola's *f.* 177.

64   [*Zola's* Son Excellence Eugène Rougon

The case of Delestang reveals to some extent the same process of creation, or grafting, if one prefers. In the novel Delestang replaces Rougon in June 1858 as Minister of the Interior. In history it was Delangle who replaced Espinasse. The names are not too different, and as Delestang is at the beginning of Zola's tale a simple member of the *Conseil d'Etat*—as had been Delangle—there is at least a certain echo here. But in this case the characters are very different. Delestang also represents Emile Ollivier's liberalism in politics,[5] which was to Zola a reflection of the Emperor's own. As Ollivier finally abandoned the Republican cause to become champion of the Liberal Empire, Republican historians of that era, bitter at what they considered to be a betrayal, lashed out at him, stating that he was mediocre (which was perhaps true) and although "honnête," "ridicule."[6] Certainly, Delestang has these characteristics. It is apparent that Zola put some of Ollivier's less admirable traits into a member of the Emperor's group, so that the Republican opposition in the novel, while not prominent, remains noble and admirable. Having settled upon the basic traits of Delestang, Zola heightened and dramatized them, as was his usual method. To portray the mediocrity of Clorinde's husband, Zola pictured him as looking extremely pensive and intelligent, as if pondering the weightiest of matters (p. 299); but in fact he is either thinking of nothing, or at the most, of what he will order for lunch. As for his "liberalism," Zola makes it clear that it is really nothing but vague sentimentality.

The development of Delestang is further complicated by Zola's statement in his worksheets (*f.* 125) that "le vrai [Eugène] Rouher, ignorant, médiocre, plaideur souple, sera le mari de mon aventurière." Despite this affirmation, De-

[5] Zola took notes on Ollivier's life. Cf. LeBlond, p. 426.
[6] *Ibid.*

lestang has so little in common with Rouher that clearly Zola must have changed his mind. Delestang's vague liberal humanitarianism is very sincere; Rouher was no liberal, and when he acted like one, it was out of pure expediency. Rouher was an excellent—if crude—orator; Delestang never appears as one. Their physical descriptions differ. While it is true that both are ignorant and mediocre people, these adjectives fit most of Zola's characters in this novel, and are not therefore sufficient to identify Rouher with Delestang. The latter emerges, then, as a mixture of Ollivier, perhaps Delangle, and fiction.

As we move up the political ladder, we encounter the Count de Marsy, whom everyone has correctly identified as the Duke de Morny. Zola occasionally interchanges their names in his worksheets (see *f*. 119), and Morny's name appears frequently throughout these notes. In Zola's initial idea, Rougon's rival was to be a vague liberal, and on *f*. 99 (early in the *ébauche*) the name Morny is crossed out and followed by that of Napoleon III himself. Was Morny such a liberal? He had been an Orleanist, and before his death in 1865 had certainly been influential in creating the Liberal Empire. Indeed, it was he who convinced Ollivier ("seduced," the Republicans say) to abandon the opposition and rally to the Emperor. But Zola was wise in not creating Marsy as a liberal Morny, for the latter's liberalism was as shallow as his Orleanism had been. Zola accepted the idea that he was above all an adventurer; the historian Albert Guérard refers to him simply as *Homo Economicus,* a spoils seeker, a judgment that history has in general supported.[7]

[7] Albert Guérard, *Napoleon III* (Cambridge, Mass., 1943), p. 226. Did Zola get confirmation of this idea in Delord (III, 54)? Here we read: "M. de Morny lui [Napoléon] fit entrevoir qu'un retour apparent aux formes des gouvernements libres, mais ne changeant rien au fond même du gouvernement personnel, ferait facilement prendre le change à l'opposition en la rassurant."

The figure of Morny had fascinated Zola for some time. When in 1870 he wrote in *La Cloche* a long letter praising Arsène Houssaye's titilative dissection of the Second Empire in his *Courtisanes du monde,* he ended his letter with a plea that Houssaye do as much in a new book for such types as Morny.[8] In his preparation for *La Conquête de Plassans,*[9] he contemplated basing a character on Morny. This interest is quite understandable, for Morny was an intriguing person. He was born in 1811, the illegitimate grandchild of Talleyrand, and the illegitimate child of Queen Hortense, and thus a bastard half-brother of Napoleon III himself; at the age of twenty-eight he had been a colonel, having served in North Africa. Later, the owner of a factory, he had become interested in agriculture, finance, and commerce. His skill became so legendary that people whispered that a financial killing could be made because "Morny est dans l'affaire." This versatile aristocrat even wrote plays. In December 1851, after a long affair with Countess LeHon, he met and married the Russian Princess Troubetzkoï, with whom, it was said, he was very much in love. Nonetheless, and despite her dazzling beauty, it was not long before he was unfaithful to her. As for Countess LeHon, she was obliged to appeal to the Emperor because Morny tried to swindle her out of money in connection with a complicated industrial enterprise which they owned jointly. The Emperor forced his half-brother to pay several million francs. In his political career he had presided over the *Corps législatif* from 1854, and, with his forceful character and aristocratic manner, did the job well. As to his death, there are two versions. The best

[8] Houssaye, a friend of Morny, was somewhat embarrassed at this misplaced praise, for he had had no idea that his frivolities would be taken so seriously. Houssaye was — as Zola himself knew — a supporter of the Empire.

[9] LeBlond ed., pp. 373, 377.

known one is that of Alphonse Daudet, who in *Le Nabab,*
gave a hideous picture of the Duke de Mora's death. Daudet
had been Morny's secretary, but that does not guarantee the
accuracy of his picture of Mora as a dissolute old rake worn
out by dangerous drugs in a desperate attempt to maintain
his virility. Ludovic Halévy, in his *Carnets,* refers to this
tale and labels it completely false.[10] He even presents Morny
as quite angelic. Whatever may be the truth of the matter,
Zola did not need to be concerned with it, for the novel ends
in 1861, four years before Morny's death.

Zola utilized Morny's life quite openly. Marsy is referred
to as a "fils de reine" (p. 77) and is forty-five years old in
1856. It is indicated (p. 78) that he is illegitimate and that
he will reign as long as the Emperor will. Zola even has
Rougon says that Marsy was born "sur les marches d'un
trône," and that "je n'ai pas grandi sous les caresses de
Tallayrand." Marsy too is a colonel at the age of twenty-
eight, then head of a factory. "On assure même qu'il a peint
des portraits et écrit des romans" (p. 77). He marries,
in January 1857, a Wallachian (Rumanian) princess—
while not Russian, she is at least Slavic—and is faithful
for barely six months (p. 149). Marsy becomes head of
the *Corps législatif* (p. 279) after the Orsini attempt. As to
his description, we read (p. 165) that he is a man with a
pale, delicate, and evil face. The photographs of Morny
tend to confirm at least the first two adjectives. Moreover,
Zola's character is active in unscrupulous deals; we have
already compared the role of Morny in the scandal of the
Grand Central Railway, with Marsy's role in Kahn's little
enterprise. The identification of Morny as Marsy is thus
thoroughly established. Zola presents Marsy as the foil to
Rougon: "la fine main gantée qui étrangle" as opposed to

[10] Paris, 1935, I, 53-61.

"le poing velu qui assomme." Robert Schnerb, in his biography of Rouher, says of Morny: "[Il] avait le tempérament du dilettante sceptique et menait la vie dissipée de profiteur du règne."[11] This description is accurate, but tends to understate Morny's political importance.

One aspect of Marsy's role in the novel may not have its origin in Morny. Marsy has written three letters to Mme de Llorentz (i.e., Countess LeHon) which in amusing fashion dissected pitilessly many highly placed people, including the Emperor himself, and the lovely lady is holding them as a weapon against him. When Clorinde seduces him, Mme de Llorentz in a fury hands the compromising letters over to Napoleon. This act shakes the Emperor's confidence in Marsy and paves the way for Rougon's return to power. Such tales of blackmail were commonly circulated at the time of Morny's marriage, when he was having difficulties with Countess LeHon. One version had Morny beg the Emperor to have his secret police destroy his letters, and indeed, the letters which had been sent to England were supposedly recovered without any scandal.[12] Frédéric Loliée spoke of the incredible stories that circulated at that time and were believed. For example, the Emperor, worrying about the revelations that would discredit many of his entourage, had urged prompt action:"Allez, agissez vite, énergiquement." Consequently,

quelques hommes de police avaient fait irruption dans l'hôtel et pénétré dans les appartements de la Comtesse LeHon. D'une voix sombre, l'un d'eux, le spadassin Grisalli, avait exigé qu'on lui livrât, sans attendre, la mystérieuse caissette renfermant les pièces secrètes et redoutées. Elle avait remis à ces gens la fameuse boîte, qui ne contenait que des lettres et qu'on alla

[11] *Rouher et le Second Empire* (Paris, 1949), p. 121.
[12] In Vicomte Beaumont-Vassy, *Histoire intime du second Empire* (Paris, 1874), pp. 182-184.

déposer, comme un précieux butin, dans le cabinet de Napoléon
III.[13]

These stories, fascinating as they may be, were apparently
without foundation. Yet it would be incorrect to assume that
such sordid melodrama was impossible under the Second
Empire. Hamel refers, with documentation, to a little problem of Auguste Billault in 1863.[14] It seems that a M. Sandon
possessed some letters in which Billault, then Minister of
the Interior, spoke very laughingly of the Emperor. To pre-
vent the exposure with which Sandon was menacing him,
the Minister had him jailed and declared insane. Hamel
quotes a letter by Persigny, who was genuinely shocked by
this conduct and wondered what to do. Fortunately for all
concerned, Billault died that year and Sandon was released.
This story is vouched for in at least two places. It is alluded
to in the *Grand Dictionnaire Universel du XIXe siècle,* under
the heading Billault. As the volume in question was published under the Empire, the article merely says that there
was a terrible scandal in Billault's life which cannot be mentioned. The new *Dictionnaire de biographie française,*[15]
under Billault, confirms this story of the

avocat de Limoges [qui] possédait de lui des lettres où il [Bil-
lault] faisait étalage d'opinions socialistes et anti-Bonapartistes.
Billault voulut les racheter. Sandon[16] refusa, mais un ami, à qui
elles avaient été confiées les apporta au ministre. Sandon fit du
bruit, engagea des procès, mais fut arrêté, enfermé à Mazas,
puis à Charenton. Persigny étouffa l'affaire.

Persigny's letter commenting on Billault's misdeed is to be
found among the papers seized at the Tuileries after the
overthow of the Empire (t. 1, p. 41). There seems little

[13] Loliée, *Les Femmes du second Empire* (Paris, 1954), pp. 210-211.
[14] III, 137-138.
[15] Paris, 1954, Vol. VI.
[16] Erroneously spelled Sandou.

doubt that Hamel copied it from these papers. In conclusion, if we have gone into such detail concerning this question of blackmailing Marsy, it is not to show that Zola used the Billault episode as a "source," which he may well not have, even if it was in Hamel; rather, it is to show that this incident does not lack verisimilitude. Government by crony and private arrangement lends itself peculiarly to these underhanded pressures, and to portray such example is a legitimate part of Zola's case against a regime which, by its very seizure of power, showed that it did not believe in the orderly process of law.

At any rate, such is Zola's Marsy: largely a carbon copy of the famous Morny,[17] but with certain traits possibly borrowed from Billault's unfortunate experience, and even from public legend. Like the other characters he is a composite, and in general the portrait is a credible one. One might object, however, that a man as astute as Marsy would be most unlikely to compromise himself by writing any such letters to a woman. He is much too cynical ever to lose his presence of mind.

The other rival to Eugène Rougon is the Italian adventuress Clorinde Balbi. F.W.J. Hemmings refers to her as a "hazily drawn adventuress of melodrama,"[18] indicating that for him Zola's creation is indeed an inferior one. It is easy to understand the critic's attitude. The fascinating wench who uses her sex to reach the top is rarely a real character, and when accompanied by Clorinde's bizarre eccentricities becomes nearly incredible. She is perhaps yet another illustration of Boileau's old maxim that "le vrai peut quelquefois n'être pas vraisemblable," for as E.M.

[17] Taxile Delord (IV, 71-72) refers to Morny as vulgar and of no real importance. This is at such variance with Zola's portrait that it seems fairly clear that Zola did not use Delord here.

[18] Hemmings, p. 70.

Grant has shown,[19] and as we shall develop further, Clorinde is in many respects patterned after the dazzling Countess of Castiglione.

Virginia Verasis, Countess of Castiglione, accompanied by her husband and small child, arrived in Paris in early 1856. She had been sent there, when only eighteen, by Count Cavour for the purpose of persuading Napoleon III, by seduction if necessary, to support a policy of Italian unification, and to combat the Papal sympathies of the Empress. All reports told of her great beauty, and she was already much talked about before making her official debut at a ball on January 29, 1856. An unbelievable spendthrift, she soon ruined her docile husband, whose despair interested her not at all. Quickly noticed by the Emperor, thanks to excellent advance publicity, she became his mistress and appeared later that fall at Compiègne for one of the week-long parties. The Imperial ardor was such that one evening when the Comédie Française was giving a performance and the Countess of Castiglione left the audience complaining of a headache, the Emperor showed the poor taste of leaving his wife shortly afterwards in order to follow her. At a dance at the Foreign Ministry on February 17, 1857, she appeared as the Queen of Hearts, in a low-cut gown which left, according to Horace de Vieil-Castel, nothing to the imagination.[20] The hearts signified her affection for the Emperor, who had made her a present of a 'chemise de nuit." That same year, her husband finally left her, and she began to experience reverses as well as triumphs. In order to pay for her extravagances, she borrowed money from the banker Lafitte and

[19] E.M. Grant, pp. 29-32.
[20] Cited by Alain Décaux, *La Castiglione: Dame de cœur de l'Europe* (Paris, 1953), p. 121. This recent biography is of prime importance because Décaux had access to Virginia's private diary.

her name was linked briefly with that of Gustav Rothschild.[21] She decided to leave Paris and was absent for some time, reappearing in 1861, at which time she settled in Passy, something of a recluse, constantly shrouded in mystery. Suddenly she would be off to Dieppe for the summer, then to Italy, or to England, sometimes rich, sometimes poor. She was suddenly invited back to the Tuileries on February 9, 1863, after an absence of five years, but the Emperor was no longer under her spell. After this failure, she let herself go, lived in semi-darkness, taking various lovers only to abandon them, emerging once to play a curious role in the Bismarck-Thiers negotiations towards the close of the Franco-Prussian War. After this last fling at politics, which had always been her primary interest to judge from Décaux's biography, she began to lose her mind, and, victim of a persecution complex, died alone in poverty in 1899.

Her character was no less strange than her career. From her earliest days she was completely spoiled.[22] She did whatever she pleased and her pride reached overweening proportions. Cynical and cold, with the greatest scorn for men, she had had several lovers before coming to France, including even King Victor Emmanuel, for one night. Her diary reveals that she wrote up her various experiences without betraying the slightest emotion. Only when presented to the King in Turin was she at all moved, and even then affected not to be.

Even as a child she was frequently untidy. "Le plancher de sa chambre se jonchait de chiffons, de robes, de fichus sortis des caisses qui arrivaient de la Sapia,"[23] and there is some evidence that at a ball in Italy she was careless of her hair-do. Yet most of the time she gave people the impression

---

[21] *Ibid.*, pp. 155-156.
[22] *Ibid.*, p. 22.
[23] *Ibid.*, p. 28.

of being a beautiful marble statue, impeccable in her groom-
ing, and extremely aloof. Eyewitnesses were in agreement,
in the words of Stéphanie Tascher de la Pagerie, that upon
her arrival in Paris she produced "l'impression d'une personne
parfaitement calme et froide préparant et ménageant ses
effets et tendant sans dévier au but qu'elle s'était proposé."[24]
Countess Stéphanie was justly noted for her powers of dis-
cernment. The general conclusion of her contemporaries, one
that modern psychologists would probably support, was that
"ce qui a toujours manqué à cette belle des belles . . . c'est
l'amour. Elle n'a jamais été aimée comme elle aurait pu
l'être parce qu'elle n'a jamais aimé qu'elle-même."[25] She was
basically frigid and her lovers complained of her coldness.

Despite her clear-headedness in acting as an agent of
Cavour, and despite the testimony of her cold, calculating
planning, she was often capricious to the point of imbalance,
especially after 1863. She would pretend to be sick, or at
other times complained of splitting headaches—often real
—and would receive her visitors while in bed, with the
covers pulled up to her nose. On other occasions she would
expose herself to her guests, limb by limb,[26] so that they
might be favored by a glimpse of perfection. Loliée recounts
that she would ask "Voulez-vous voir mon bras?"[27] Later
on in her life, she decorated her room with black rugs and
black paper, so that the whiteness of her skin would create
a magnificent contrast (p. 64). But as time passed, her
quarters, never very neat, became more and more untidy,
and were always in need of a good cleaning.

[24] *Ibid.*, p. 106.
[25] She enjoyed looking at herself in the mirror. Décaux gives a
description of her in 1856: "Grands yeux bleus, bouche petite, joli nez,
cheveux noirs aux reflets fauves encadrant un visage mat, son corps
mince, sa poitrine haute et ferme" (p. 81).
[26] *Ibid.*, p. 210.
[27] *Les Femmes du second Empire*, p. 71.

There are no notes in Zola's worksheets that refer either
directly or indirectly to "la Castiglione," and for some reason Zola appeared unwilling to divulge his source for Clorinde Balbi,[28] but it is evident that the novelist has re-created
this magnificent adventuress. As the Parisian of the Second
Empire knew little about her origins, Zola, unable to learn
much himself, wrote of her early years with planned confusion. He invented or set down several vague, conflicting
stories and eliminated the husband and the child, for his plot
required a woman free to marry, and the presence of the child
would detract from her glamour. At any rate, Clorinde
arrives in Paris at Cavour's request at about the same date
and at the same age as her historical counterpart. The novelist alludes discreetly to a liaison with "un très haut per-
sonnage," (p. 60) although in the novel it is not the daughter
but the mother who is referred to here. If this vague al-
lusion, on which one cannot rely completely, means that
Zola knew of Virginia's affair with the future King of Italy,
it is likely that he did not use it in its original form because
it is hard to believe and especially because he wished his adventuress to start from the bottom of the ladder and work
her way up by degrees to the bed of the Emperor.[29]

Once in Paris, like the historical Countess, Clorinde goes
to the dance at the Ministry of Foreign Affairs; she is also
mentioned (pp. 17, 66) as having attend a ball at the Italian
legation in the diaphanous costume of Diana, the Huntress.
There seems to be here an echo of the rumor that "la Castiglione" had appeared at a dance clad in the transparent veils
of Salammbô. Actually, on that one occasion, she was mod-

---

[28] Jan Ten Brink in his correspondence with Zola (N.A.F. 24512,
letters of Dec. 7, 1876, July 12, 1877, May 16, 1879, and July 25, 1879),
kept asking who the model for Clorinde was. Apparently Zola never
answered the question, even though Ten Brink finally guessed the truth.
[29] The worksheets repeatly refer to Clorinde's rise by "étapes."

estly dressed. Venomous tongues confused her with another woman who had gone dressed as Flaubert's heroine. But it was widely believed that the Countess had been thus attired and the novelist no doubt heard the story. As *Salammbô* did not appear until 1862, Zola could not use the incident in his novel; hence, perhaps, the change to Diana. At any rate, Clorinde is also mentioned as appearing as the Queen of Hearts "dans un bal . . . au ministère de la marine . . . avec des cœurs de diamants à son cou, à ses poignets, à ses genoux" (p. 318).[30] There are also references to her sudden disappearances and reappearances with her fortune remade (p. 60).

Her character, with one interesting exception, is also a faithful representation of that of the Countess. Zola paints her as basically unintelligent, except for her ability to handle men. Her favorite book — she reads very little —is *Léonora la Bohémienne,* which she read when young. The plot is indeed juvenile: a girl, captured by bandits, marries a lord at the end of the story. According to Abel Hermant,[31] la Castiglione's favorite reading was *Ildegonsa,* an equally idiotic tale of a nun in love fleeing a convent, who ultimately dies at the stake, having received grace to resist her lover. As a point of fact, the Countess was very superstitious, but not at all religious. It is here that the anticlerical Zola makes an error. To show her lack of intelligence and her superstition, he can think of no better way than to make her devout to the point of bigotry. She therefore appears as hypersensitive on religious matters and flies into a rage when a crucifix is accidentally broken. She even has a previous recollection of an audience with the Pope, who called her his "little apostle," and for whom she has the greatest awe and

[30] A similarity first pointed out by E.M. Grant, *op. cit.,* p. 32.
[31] *La Castiglione: La dame de cœur des Tuileries* (Paris, 1938), p. 35.

reverence. The difficulty is that if she were so attached to the Pope, she would never have allowed herself to become Cavour's agent, bustling around Paris on countless errands of political intrigue, trying to persuade Napoleon III to support Italian unification at the expense of the Pope's temporal possessions.[32]

As to the frigidity of his notorious adventuress, Zola reverted once more to history. Indeed, he made a special point of it. When Clorinde dresses up to make a conquest, she sighs wearily: "Il le faut bien" (p. 201), and Zola adds: "Elle y mettait si peu de plaisir." She comments that "quand on parlait de quelque femme dont on ne comptait plus les amants, elle ouvrait de grands yeux d'enfant, des yeux surpris, en demandant: 'ça l'amuse donc?'" (p. 153). Clorinde has the same scorn for men that Virginia Verasis had.[33] She too indulges in narcissistic adoration of her body. It is no wonder then that men acted slightly frightened of the two.[34]

When it came to her caprices, Zola copied directly once more. "Elle avait eu, un soir, l'étonnante fantaisie de faire tendre sa chambre de draperies noires semées de larmes d'argent, et de recevoir ses intimes, couchée sur son lit, ensevelie dans des couvertures, également noires, qui ne laissaient passer que le bout de son nez" (p. 18). The only discrepancy, historically speaking, in this detail is that Zola placed in 1856 a trait that seemed to have developed later on. Her exhibitionism, a form of scorn that consisted of casting pearls before real swine, is frequently mentioned by

[32] Loliée, *op. cit.*, p. 34, speaks of her as "lancée quotidiennement au trot de ses chevaux, et tenant sur les genoux un portefeuille bourré de notes, de documents, de brochures . . . ." Clorinde's briefcase is always similarly stuffed.

[33] Loliée, p. 27, attributes to her a statement that she equaled all men by her birth, surpassed them in beauty, and judged them with her mind.

[34] Zola, *SEER*, p. 184.

Zola. Not only do we see the fair lady exposed like a marble statue at the time of Rougon's first visit to her quarters, but also when the banker Reuthlinger, a suggestion of the Countess' financial friends, visits her to receive political information, she exposes herself calmly in his presence[35] and shows him nearly to the door before becoming aware of her nudity and blushing for it.

Toward the end of the novel, Zola gives another description of her apartment:

La chambre elle-même, autrefois mauve tendre, passée aujourd'hui au gris sale, restait comme pleine de buée suspendue; on distinguait à peine des coins de fauteuils arrachés des traînées de poussière sur les meubles, une large tache d'encre étalée au beau milieu du tapis, quelque encrier tombé là, qui avait éclaboussé les boiseries; au fond, les rideaux du lit étaient tirés, sans doute pour cacher le désordre des couvertures (p. 330).

The similarity with the following description of the quarters of the Countess of Castiglione is striking. A notary who visited her apartment on the Place Vendôme reported:

Une vieille domestique me fit entrer enfin (sans doute la nourrice italienne ramenée de Florence) dans une anti-chambre obscure, puis dans un salon bas, où derrière les volets clos, on se cognait dans les meubles . . . posés là au milieu d'un désordre . . . . Tout était poussiéreux . . . et partout dans cet entresol, flottait un air enfermé . . . . Tout était fané, négligé, sans aucune trace de soins ménagers ou de propreté élémentaire. Cette pièce était dans le même désordre que le reste du logis. Des vêtements, dentelles, fourrures, étaient jetés sur les meubles, parmi les étoffes. Je vis alors Mme de Castiglione à demi-couchée sur son lit, vêtue d'un manteau doublé d'hermine et, il m'a semblé, sans linge . . . . Elle me reçut fort mal, occupée à écrire sur ses

[35] Décaux, p. 117, quotes Mme de Metternich as saying that one did not become surprised at Mme de Castiglione's nudity because she resembled an ancient statue: "Le décolletage, quoique excessif, ne paraissait pas indécent, tant cette superbe créature ressemblait à une statue antique."

genoux avec un crayon et sur un livre qui lui servait de bu-
vard.[36]

Since Madame de Castiglione moved to her apartment
on the Place Vendôme after Zola wrote *Son Excellence
Eugène Rougon,* the novelist could not have been familiar
with it when writing his novel, but no matter where one
moves, one soon lives according to one's character, and it
seems most likely that his description might fit Mme de
Castiglione's lodgings on the Rue Nicolo in Passy.[37] Of
course, if we compare the notary's description with the one
given by Zola, we find one noticeable difference. There is,
in the latter, only disorder, but not decay. The difference
would be explained by the lapse in time: Clorinde is young
and full of life; Mme de Castiglione was twenty years older
than when she first came to Paris.

It is through this description that we may discover where
Zola possibly obtained much of his information on his adventuress. As a young man, Bac had the privilege of listening to the fascinating recollections of Arsène Houssaye and
of General Fleury,[38] and it is the former who reported in
greatest detail on the Countess. Zola knew Houssaye personally, although not intimately, and had even been invited
to the latter's "mardis" on the Avenue Friedland.[39]   One
cannot be sure that it was Houssaye who supplied the naturalist with the piquant biographical details, but it is far from
impossible.[40]

[36] F. Bac, *Intimités du second Empire: la cour et la ville* (Paris, 1931), p. 25.
[37] The lodgings no longer exist.
[38] There is some information on her in *Souvenirs du Général Comte Fleury* (Paris, 1898), cited by E.M. Grant, p. 31.
[39] L. Auriant, "E. Zola et les deux Houssaye. Documents inédits," *Mercure de France,* June 1940, pp. 555-569.
[40] Houssaye's own "novels," or racy tales, have in them no obvious traits of "la Castiglione" used either by Zola or mentioned in Décaux or elsewhere.

There is still another trait of Clorinde's that might well have had its origin in Houssaye. We have already mentioned her posing without any embrarrassment and then suddenly blushing as she realized her nudity when showing the banker to the door. Similarly in Chapter III of the novel she suddenly becomes aware of her exposure in front of Rougon and covers herself quickly (p. 71). The journalist Jules Hoche, writing about 1881, tells a story with which Arsène Houssaye had entertained him. The text indicates that the scene took place some years previously:

Tel portrait de femme . . . étalant une nudité sculpturale et dont la pudeur n'est habillée que d'un loup noir, est celui d'une femme du monde, ange déchu aujourd'hui et dont les secrètes perversions se trahissaient alors déjà par des fantaisies bizarres. L'une de ces fantaisies la poussa un jour à soutenir devant Arsène Houssaye que le courage de livrer sa nudité au pinceau ne lui paraissait pas difficile même pour une femme honnête. Arsène Houssaye la prit au mot. Elle accepta le défi crânement, et posa, sans voile aucun, sur le lit même de l'auteur. La séance se passa sans que la femme parût éprouver la moindre émotion. Mais ce fut autre chose quand il fallut se lever et se rhabiller. Au premier mouvement de son corps, elle eut conscience de sa nudité et son visage devint pourpre.

Houssaye concludes philosophically that it is the motion of the body that changes the statue into the naked woman.[41]

In spite of some obvious similarites, it is far from certain that Houssaye's model was the Countess herself, but it is not hard to imagine the voluble Houssaye telling this tale many a time (even if he invented it in the first place) and as it fits the Countess' well-known exhibitionism, Zola would merely have had to embellish it a little and fit it into his novel. All this is very speculative, of course, but even if Zola did not take this detail directly from Houssaye, he may

[41] Jules Hoche, *Les Parisiens chez eux* (Paris, 1883), p. 310.

have heard it or a similar tale elsewhere. Regardless of the source, however, this audacious posing was not unknown to the last half of the nineteenth century; consequently Zola's portrait is not so lacking in verisimilitude as one might at first be tempted to suspect.

The final detail—the ornate collar that Clorinde receives from the Emperor, bearing the inscription: "J'appartiens à mon maître," with a gold bell containing a pearl— is without doubt fictional. Mention of it in the histories and memoirs of the period seems impossible to find, and such a dramatic and provocative gift could hardly have escaped the notice of the eager chroniclers of the age. Of course, this detail is most consistent with the character both of Virginia Verasis[42] and of Clorinde Balbi, and in the case of the latter, it comes as a fitting culmination of her ascension. In this way Zola dramatized in unforgettable fashion his remarkable historical re-creation of a woman who was for a moment the center of everyone's attention in Parisian society, and at the same time, like Nana later on, a symbol of its frenetic immorality.

We arrive finally at Eugène Rougon himself, the focal personage of the novel. He had already appeared in the first novel of the series, *La Fortune des Rougon*. To consider only the adult Eugène, he was nearly forty years old in 1848 and, according to the heredity that Zola planned for him, represented a simple mixture, both in appearance and in character:

C'était un garçon de taille moyenne, légèrement chauve, tournant déjà à l'obésité. Il avait le visage de son père, un visage long aux traits larges; sous la peau on devinait la graisse qui amollissait les rondeurs et donnait à la face une blancheur jaunâtre

[42] Of her Mérimée said, "[Elle] proclamait son impudeur comme un flagrant délit qu'elle eût provoqué sur elle-même." F. Bac, *Intimités du second Empire*, p. 32.

de cire. Mais si l'on sentait encore le paysan dans la structure massive de sa tête, la physionomie se transfigurait, s'éclairait au dedans, lorsque le regard s'éveillait en soulevant les paupières appesanties. Chez le fils, la lourdeur du père était devenue gravité. Ce gros garçon avait d'ordinaire une attitude de sommeil puissant; à certains gestes larges et fatigués on eût dit un géant qui se détirait les membres en attendant l'action.[43]

As to his goals, Zola is equally clear: "Il avait des ambitions hautes, des instincts autoritaires, un mépris singulier pour les petits moyens et les petites fortunes" (p. 74). The novelist then speaks of his "besoin de domination," his "voix pâteuse" and "geste lourd."[44] In short, Eugène has exactly the temperament and manner that he will reveal in *Son Excellence Eugène Rougon.* As for his early career, Eugène is a poor country lawyer who often loses cases because he enjoys practicing oratory in court rather than working for his client. He then goes to Paris, where he becomes a Bonapartist agent, helping to prepare the coup d'état. He reappears briefly in *La Curée,* where he is referred to as being "une puissance occulte" (p. 52) in 1852 and then a deputy (p. 57). Thus when Zola began his new novel, he already had a character made to order.

Who is Rougon's historical prototype? We have already mentioned—as indeed have most recent critics—that for a moment he can be identified with General Espinasse, and in the final chapter he fulfils the political role of Eugène Rouher, who would later rise to the exalted status of Vice-Emperor. But it would be best to start at the beginning. The *ébauche* of *Son Excellence Eugène Rougon* indicates that although Zola had already outlined Rougon's character in his first novel of the *Rougon-Macquart,* he wished to pattern

[43] *La Fortune des Rougon,* p. 73.
[44] The genealogical tree, which dated from 1870, states: *"Mélange fusion.* Prépondérance morale de sa mère. Ressemblance physique du père."

him after some historical figure. In his notes (*f. 267*) Zola
established a momentary parallel with Guizot:

Un ambitieux (Guizot), modération hardie, volonté énergique.
La responsabilité l'attirait. Très brave dans la lutte. Il se
possédait, voyait, entendait, au milieu de la mêlée parlementaire.
Il n'hésitait jamais à monter à la Tribune. Fermeté des convictions, allant à l'inflexibilité provocante. Un croyant déter-
miné. Ne se pliait pas aux faits accomplis . . . . (Un type
d'ambitieux parallèle ou contraire *à créer*).

It is evident here that Zola was seeking an historical figure
who would fit the preconceived idea that he had for his
statesman-to-be in *La Fortune des Rougon*. Whether the
original idea itself was based on an historical character is
impossible to determine. The notes for that first novel give
no indication. The chances are that it was not.

Guizot apparently did not seem to suit the novelist's
needs, perhaps because of the firmness of his convictions,
and Zola looked elsewhere. He has biographical notes on
Persigny, Billault, Baroche, Fould, Ollivier and Morny as
well as on Rouher. On *f.* 125 we read, however, "Ne pas
oublier que je fais un Rouher très grandi."[45] The similarity
of the family name is a pure coincidence. Paul Raphaël has
shown that Zola took the name from a schoolmate.[46] As to
the name Eugène, Zola declared: "J'ai pris le prénom
d'Eugène absolument par hasard . . ."[47]

The German critic Keins has suggested that some scholars have gone too far in equating Rouher and Rougon.[48]
Keins points out that Persigny might well be a component

---

[45] It is here that he suggests that the real Rouher was to be Delestang,
as we have mentioned above. As we shall show, Rougon is far closer
to the real Rouher than this statement would suggest.

[46] "*La Fortune des Rougon* et la réalité historique," *Mercure de
France*, Oct. 1, 1923.

[47] F. Xau, *Emile Zola* (Paris, 1880), p. 45. The same conclusion is
reached by LeBlond, p. 406.

[48] Keins, *op. cit.*

part of the fictional creation, for this minister fell from grace in 1854 and returned to power in 1861. He suggests that Zola might have changed the first date in order to begin the novel with the scene of the baptism. Otherwise, the date approximates Rougon's rise and fall. Keins also mentions Persigny's authoritarian temperament as being similar to that of Zola's creation. Keins might have added too that Rougon's abortive studies concerning a parallel between the English and French constitutions are reminiscent of such a study made by Persigny,[49] in which the former ambassador to the Court of Saint James tried to prove, like Rougon in the novel, that the French were as free as the English.[50] But in the end Keins, like most French critics, considers Rougon a composite figure and a symbol of the Minister of State under Napoleon III. It is easy to agree with this interpretation when one reads the lives of the various political leaders of the regime. Of Baroche, for instance, Zola wrote in his notes: "Laborieux, souple, rabaissant les questions, prêt à parler sur tout, inépuisable, vulgaire."[51] As for Billault, he concocted the authoritarian election circulars which have already been mentioned. Surely these various traits fit Rougon, at least in part.

A close examination of the life of Eugène Rouher, however, reveals some interesting parallels to the life of Rougon. One must make it clear from the outset that Zola was in no way trying to make an accurate biography of Rouher. Many aspects of the latter's life differ sharply from Rougon's. Yet Rouher's biographer Robert Schnerb, referring to Zola's novel, states that Rougon is a Rouher "mi-historique."[52]

[49] Cited by Delord, III, 399-400.
[50] *Ibid.*, V, 263-264, quotes Persigny complaining to Napoleon about the lack of a firm hand to guide the country's destiny. Rougon thinks identically and says as much many times.
[51] LeBlond, p. 425.
[52] *Op. cit.*, p. 331.

According to Schnerb, Rouher, like Rougon, was a vigorous
man who retained his peasant characteristics (pp. 12, 165)
and showed no disposition for the arts. He married into the
world of government officials and, upon arrival in Paris, at
first lived very cheaply. "On l'avait connu besogneux.
Lebey, un de ses compagnons de la première heure, arrivé
dans l'industrie, s'était écrié : 'Eh quoi ! Rouher ministre?
Rouher que j'ai vu, moi, déjeuner à treize sous chez Rou-
get' " (p. 150). We are certainly not far from the wearisome monologues of Gilquin to the Charbonnels, as he
reminds them (p. 95) that Rougon and he had started off
humbly together.

Perhaps because of the slender means of the Rouher
family, their life was quiet and decent.

Maupas, qui le déteste, se porte garant de l'honnêteté de ses
moeurs. "M. Rouher, écrit-il, vivait simplement en bon père de
famille. Le soir, après le dîner, il s'accordait le plaisir de quelques parties de whist ou de piquet; il aimait à faire des réussites
. . . .[53] Quelques rares et très sûrs amis pénétraient seuls dans
son intimité . . . . Mme Rouher menait bien son intérieur."[54]

Except for the fact that Rougon's friends are not very reliable, the description is that of a "jeudi" at Rougon's house,
exact even to the solitaire. Rouher liked a quiet evening at
home, and found gala parties, concerts, dances a torture—
even at the Tuileries.[55] In Zola's novel, Clorinde feels that
she must push Rougon into accepting the invitation to Compiègne. As to Rouher' wife, Schnerb writes : "On fut long-
temps sans la connaître à la cour" (p. 154) and in *Son
Excellence Eugène Rougon,* the Emperor thoughtfully inquires after Rougon's sick wife (p. 167) although it is ob-

[53] A detail mentioned by E.M. Grant, p. 38, and in LeBlond, p. 406.
[54] Schnerb, p. 149.
[55] *Ibid.,* p. 153.

vious that her illness is only a pretext. She has no desire to appear at court.

In the political world, Rouher, too, had his "gang," mostly relatives for whom he found jobs in his native Auvergne. We have already alluded to Rougon's complete lack of convictions in the realm of ideas, except for his scorn of anything genuinely parliamentary. Rouher, too, had little use for parliamentarianism, according to his biographer (p. 161). Like Rougon, the real-life politician had no patience with the concept of the new nobility that Napoleon wished to create (p. 166). As for censorship, we have seen Rougon at work, personally supervising the press. Normally the Minister of the Interior did not, indeed could not, supervise the newspapers personally. There were various intermediaries who brought questionable articles to his attention. But Rouher, too, was made of stern stuff: "De fait, il se tient au courant de l'activité que déploie le service de la presse et de la librairie, rattaché à l'Intérieur; il suit de près le tirage des différentes feuilles . . ." (pp. 167-168). Such work must have been tiring, for Rouher was often weary: "Les symptômes de lassitude se précisaient plus nombreux à partir de 1866, dus non seulement aux déceptions, mais à des causes physiologiques" (p. 154). Zola constantly refers to Rougon's heavy-lidded lassitude.

When it came to economic affairs, Rouher had a keen mind. At the Emperor's request, he was instrumental in creating a new free-trade treaty with Britain in 1860. This detail does not appear in the novel, but other parallels between the two men are discernible. The reader will recall Rougon's desire to found a model farming community in the Landes, where he could rule as dictator. Rouher had similar interests, although probably a different motivation. A law passed in 1857, aimed at reforesting the Landes, was a prelude to the national plans of 1860 and 1864.[56] In a report of January 13, 1860, Rouher submitted a plan for a vast program affecting nearly 7½ million hectares in all. In the novel the Emperor ponders uncertainly whether to retain Rougon in Paris in the case of a political emergency. In the light of that attitude, we may meditate on this note from Fould to Baroche in 1864:

Ce sont les dernières conversations que l'Empereur aura avec Rougon qui le fixeront sur le parti à prendre. Il est clair qu'il y a dans son esprit un combat entre le sentiment de la nécessité du concours de Rouher et l'inquiétude de lui donner une trop grande prépondérance.[57]

One might object that all the above-mentioned parallels could simply be the result of coincidence or that they arise purely from the nature of the jobs held by Rouher and Rougon, for there is admittedly no confirmation to be found in Zola's worksheets. But when we consider Rouher's oratorical delivery, we find an exactness of detail so great that coincidence is out of the question. Schnerb, utilizing various accounts of the time, describes Rouher at the speaker's rostrum in great detail. According to one eyewitness account: "Il parle mal, très mal. Il n'a pas de voix. Il broie du mortier. Les sons passent éraillés dans une gorge épuisée" (p. 136), and there is also a reference to Rouher's "pâteux patois" (p. 135). But once warmed up, Rouher could talk at great length. Emile Ollivier wrote: "Pendant des heures, [il] ferrailla, exposa, raconta, d'un ton d'une extraordinaire vigueur, en orateur de premier ordre, soulevant d'une main toujours alerte le fardeau d'un entassement d'idées pas toujours bien digérées et classées" (p. 136). The orator was renowned for his "argument massif," and "absence de sentiment littéraire" (p. 142). Schnerb judges that the "Vice-

[56] *Ibid.,* pp. 72-73.   [57] *Ibid.,* pp. 154-155.

Emperor" was no writer, but if his speeches may have seemed crude, they were nonetheless clever and powerful: "Il met une véritable affection à reconstituer le raisonnement qu'il propose de ruiner. Il lui arrive de reprendre mot pour mot, intonation pour intonation, les phrases de l'adversaire" (p. 140). De Maupas wrote:

La forme, due tout entière à l'improvisation, était élégante, puissante à l'occasion; elle trahissait volontiers comme une sorte d'émotion pathétique qui produisait un effet considérable sur ceux qui ignoraient que cette émotion était purement artificielle, et seulement l'un des moyens favoris du Ministre d'Etat. Cette ressource, tant soit peu dramatique, M. Rouher la mettait en œuvre surtout dans ses repliques, dont la forme pompeuse faisait le principal mérite.[58]

And Halévy stated: "Il y a souvent de la lourdeur et de la vulgarité dans cette éloquence, mais c'est de l'éloquence tout de même. Il fallait à tout prix donner les coups de poing à la fin, et ils ont été vigoureusement assénés."[59] To reinforce his words, Rouher used gestures that fit his heavy physique. "Il avait le physique de l'homme qui se sent sûr de lui . . . une sorte de force animale le servait. Il n'était pas de haute stature mais bien planté sur des jambes courtes portant un buste massif."[60] The testimony of those who heard him centered largely on gestures made with his hands, referring to "cette main faite pour saisir solidement le rebord de la tribune ou pour se fermer en un poing volumineux, apte à tomber comme un marteau sur la table" (p. 137). Another description reads:

Rouher n'avait pas le geste continu. L'habitude de tendre les bras en avant, de replier les doigts sur la paume de la main sauf à braquer l'index sur l'ennemi, l'allure de sanglier qui se ramasse pour bondir, l'usage du coup de poing sur la table pour

[58] *Mémoires sur le second Empire* (Paris, 1884-5), v. 2, p. 217.
[59] Schnerb, p. 133.
[60] *Ibid.*, p. 136.

ponctuer, tout cela sentait le mélodrame et choquait les délicats.
(p. 138).

Claveau reported that when Rouher became angry, "le
cou s'enflait comme celui du taureau prêt à donner de la
corne" (p. 137).

Where did Zola get his information on Rouher? There
is no reference anywhere to direct sources. We know that
Zola did see Rouher when the latter was a deputy at Versailles
in 1872, but the novelist barely mentioned him.[61] Let us
watch Rougon in action in the final chapter as he replies (p.
393) to the attacks of the opposition. "Rougon, les épaules ar-
rondies, était monté pesamment à la tribune . . . il posait
devant lui un paquet de notes, . . . promenait ses mains,
comme pour prendre possession de l'étroite caisse d'acajou.
Enfin, adossé au bureau, au fond, il leva la face." He begins
to speak in his "langue lourde et pâteuse." As he develops
his points, he becomes stronger (p. 394). Maintenant, le
corps un peu penché, le bras droit tendu, il haussait la voix
. . . ." After an interruption by the opposition (p. 395), "il
apaisa la Chambre d'un geste; et s'appuyant des deux poings
au bord de la tribune, il se tourna vers la gauche, d'un air
de sanglier acculé." As for Rougon's oratorical methods:

Bien qu'il eût promis de ne pas réfuter le discours du député

[61] At the time, Zola was a reporter for *La Cloche,* and he witnessed
daily sessions of the legislature at Versailles. These articles have been
collected in *La République en marche: Chroniques parlementaires,* 2
Tomes, ed. Jacques Kayser (Paris: Fasquelle, 1956). Rouher appears but
briefly in one article (II, 174) portrayed in two brief sentences as a
wreck of his former self. It was the first time Zola had seen him. The
brief sketch of Rouher here cannot have served for the novel, for in
Zola's newspaper articles, Rouher never speaks. More generally, the
articles of Zola for *La Cloche* provide only the most general background
for the novel. Certain descriptions of the interior of the legislature do
perhaps anticipate *SEER* (I, 65), but that is all. The only important
aspect of these chronicles is to record Zola's growing distaste for parle-
mentary wrangling, which probably explains in part Zola's cynicism on
the subject in Chapter i.

de la gauche, il entra ensuite dans une discussion minutieuse. Il
fit d'abord un exposé très complet des arguments de son adversaire; il y mettait une sorte de coquetterie . . . . Son grand corps
emplissait la tribune. Ses épaules, balancées, suivaient le roulis
de ses phrases. Il avait l'éloquence banale, incorrecte . . . enflant
les lieux communs, les faisant crever en coup de foudre. Il ton-
nait, il brandissait des mots bêtes. Sa seule supériorité d'orateur
était son haleine . . . berçant les périodes, coulant magnifique-
ment pendant des heures.

As the hours pass, Rougon approaches the climax (p. 398):

Il empoignait le bois de la tribune de ses doigts crispés. Il jetait
son corps en avant, balayait l'air de son bras droit . . . . Brusquement . . . il parut pris d'une fureur haletante. Son poing
tendu, lancé en manière de bélier, menaçait quelque chose, là-
bas, dans le vide.

Then the orator softens his tone, speaks highly of Napoleon III, and sits down. Shortly afterwards, however, he has
to speak again:

Rougon, la nuque encore mouillée de sueur, la voix enrouée,
son grand corps brisé par son premier discours, s'entêta à
répondre tout de suite. Ce fut un beau spectacle. Il étala sa
fatigue, la mit en scène, se traîna à la tribune, où il balbutia
d'abord des paroles éteintes. . . . il leur parlait avec une humilité
pleine de ruse . . . Mais peu à peu, sa voix avait repris toute
son emphase. Il emplissait la salle de son mugissement, il se
tapait la poitrine à grands coups de poing (p. 400).

He triumphs magnificently, if cynically. It is clear that word
by word, gesture by gesture, Rougon as an orator is modeled
after Rouher.

Thus Rougon is in his exterior manifestations Rouher,
except for a brief pause to assume to aspect of General
Espinasse. The only difference between fact and fiction, other
than Zola's normal tendency to exaggerate a little, is the
whole matter of his relationship with Clorinde Balbi. This

creation is fictional, for Rouher and Mme de Castiglione never had any dealings with each other. Angus Wilson has suggested that Zola used his own temperament here.[62] This suggestion, first proposed by Paul Alexis[63] is quite plausible. The massive, bull-like Rougon evokes, at least to some extent, the powerful, driving Zola who feared and did not understand provocative women, yet was strongly attracted to them underneath. If correct, this theory may help to explain the tremendous force in Rougon that is vital in sustaining a novel that might easily have become bogged down in the sordid pettiness of its plot.

Despite Zola's partial self-portrait in Rougon, the latter, like Clorinde and Marsy, to mention only the principal personages of the novel, is an historical evocation. If we have gone to considerable pains to establish the very numerous parallels between fictional character and historical counterpart, it has been to show that in this novel Zola quite intentionally refused to create any major characters who were independent beings. It is of course true that the character whose inner life gives him an autonomy which removes him from the complete control of his creator—the author—is rare in the *Rougon-Macquart* cycle. Zola created from the outside, that is from the situation, controlling his characters in accordance with his plot needs and also with his deterministic view of life.[64] In *Son Excellence Eugène Rougon,* Zola followed his normal tendency even more than usual. As a result, it is easy to evaluate his success in this type of character creation.

One of the most common ways of composing an historical novel has been to create a fictional individual who will,

[62] Wilson, *Emile Zola,* pp. 42-43.

[63] *Emile Zola, notes d'un ami* (Paris, 1882), p. 105. Cited by LeBlond, p. 406.

[64] Buteau in *La Terre* and Etienne Lantier in *Germinal* are perhaps two notable exceptions.

in his adventures, come into contact with the main historical figures figures of his day who will judge the good and the bad as he pursues, and usually conquers, his lady love. In this type of novel, *à la* Scott, the hero and heroine can be entirely fictional—and are usually quite two-dimensional —and the others may be presented as they would be by an historian. In refusing to adopt this form and in writing about recent history and many people who were still alive, Zola was forced to create characters who were three things at once. For the originality of the plot, there would have to be original creation. Thus it is that Rougon's relation- ship with his clique and with Clorinde is sheer fiction, as is Clorinde's desire to promote her husband to power. Yet into these same characters Zola had to fuse recognizable political prototypes because of his intention to expose the defects of the Second Empire. Hence the extraordonary correlation of Rougon, Marsy, and Clorinde with Rouher, Morny, and the Countess of Castiglione. Finally, these fictional historical characters had to be symbolic of types. Zola succeeds with Rougon, combining in him many of the attributes of Persigny, as well as those of Rouher and Espinasse. In Marsy, Zola has represented not only Morny, but also the elegant débauché of the mid-nineteenth century, the speculator profiting from the capitalistic and govern- mental ventures of the day. Clorinde Balbi is perhaps less symbolic. We remember Hemmings' dismissal of her as an unbelievable creation. Because of her incredible eccentricities, she is not quite symbolic of the women who tempted the Emperor. Zola might have created a more representative figure in choosing some other of Napoleon's mistresses, but one finds it difficult to blame him for selecting the notorious Countess, particularly when he must have known that many a reader in 1876 would remember her and feel the truth, not the exaggeration, of his portrait. If a novelist wishes to create a character who is at the same time biographically accurate, historically representative, and fictionally original, he must exercise the greatest control from beginning to end. The slightest degree of autonomy, or self-development, by the character will inevitably destroy at least part of the triple equation. Since Zola needed all three aspects to make a sound historical novel, as he envisaged it, he cannot be blamed for his choice of method. Quite the contrary, in *Son Excellence Eugène Rougon,* biography, history, and invention blend smoothly.

There are, perhaps, two dangers implicit in such a method of creation. The first is that since the character is a composite of history and fiction, the author—or should one say the arranger?—may make a mistake, creating some contradiction with the character or with the history of the time. As we have already seen, Zola perhaps made one in the case of Marsy, hardly a man to write incriminating letters. He certainly erred in the case of Clorinde, whose religiosity was in conflict with her actions as an agent of Cavour. It is always possible that a character who is put together to satisfy the author's needs for plot, structure, and ideas may be guilty of that type of inconsistency. Of course, we do not mean to imply that conversely all attempts to create a character who develops as an independent creation are necessarily successful. Such a one may be a total failure. But if he did manifest any inconsistencies, the author would no doubt attempt to explain them by some basic tension that lay behind them. His weakness would not be those of some of Zola's characters.

The other danger in such a method of creation is that the character, who is obliged to be three things at once: a symbol, a fragment of history, and a part of the plot, often does not come to life or arouse the deepest interest. This criticism may, I believe, be leveled at nearly all of Zola's novels, which are social rather than individual.[65] Indeed, it can be leveled at the naturalistic novel itself, which, in opposite fashion to the metaphysical novel, tends to minimize to protagonist in favor of a class or all society. We might well expect such a slackening of interest in *Son Excellence Eugène Rougon,* when we consider the lack of epic grandeur which breathes life into such novels as *Germinal* and *La Terre.* But despite the petty, sordid world of politics, the novel sustains the reader to the end. This is possible only because of the character of Rougon. We have attempted to show how closely it is based on historical counterparts, but the reader must sense that there is something else too. There is a spring of desire and frustration, a tremendous, barely restrained power that dominates the book. The most obvious explanation of this power is that the suspicions of Jouvenel (see above, p. 33), Hemmings, Wilson, etc. are correct: that Zola has poured his own very real repressed urges into Rougon and thus has animated him in a way that is not true of the others. This animation lifts Rougon from the ranks of the mediocre characters and gives him the fascination that he possesses.

Rougon is put into even bolder relief through Zola's able presentation of the dozen or so minor characters who form the great man's clique, and who gives to the novel a magnificent background. They have the requisite flat, gray qualities to silhouette the main characters, but simultaneously, in sometimes combatting Rougon's actions, they take on their own motion and reality which give them the vigor that they need. These nonentities might at first glance seem unworthy of such extensive analysis. They have no traceable historical

---

[65] Some of Zola's novels are great, but usually for reasons other than those of characterization.

prototypes; it is probable that they are entirely fictional. As we observe them, they are certainly not developed characters in any genuine sense. We have already seen some of them in action. They reveal themselves only as grasping hands, as itching palms, with few details of their personal lives. Yet we shall see that it would be a grave mistake to neglect them. To begin with, a brief sketch of each is in order.

Du Poizat, at the beginning of the story, is the subprefect at Bressuire, in the department of Deux-Sèvres. He is only thirty years old, but already he seems aged and bitter. He had known poverty in Paris because his avaricious father gave him but a pittance. Querulous and vicious, he is described as Rougon's "ancien lieutenant, dont les dents blanches mal rangées ressemblaient à celles d'un jeune loup" (p. 35).

There is M. Bouchard, sixty years of age, worn out from twenty-five years of administrative toil. A most mediocre man, he has been passed over several times for advancement, and is openly seeking Rougon's assistance. He has made the mistake of marrying a young country girl in order to make sure that he will have a wife who will remain faithful to him, unlike those immoral Parisian girls. She has decieved him abominably and at the moment is seeking the advancement of her lover, young d'Escorailles, whom Rougon has had appointed six months previously to a position with the Conseil d'Etat. The parents of the young man, the Marquis d'Escorailles and his wife, despite their legitimist railings against the Second Empire, are perfectly willing that their son should advance, and are most respectful to Rougon —until he falls from power.

The military is present also. Colonel Jobelin, a retired officer, is seeking a job for his son Auguste. The lad is only fifteen and cannot pass the required examinations, but to

please the colonel, Rougon manages to bypass them and is
later sharply criticized for his action. The boy himself is
something of a young delinquent who spends most of his time
slinking around Clorinde's apartment, sniffing her perfumes
and negligees.

We have already referred to the Charbonnels. While they
are seeking to recapture an inheritance from the Church,
they are nonetheless outwardly very respectful of the pro-
prieties, always ready with a good word for conservative,
established institutions, but at heart, ever ready to forget
these pious utterances when their own interests are at stake.
This couple is less aggressive than many of the others of the
clique, but for this reason Rougon seems to feel even more
obligated than usual to help them, because they rely upon
his promises. More than once he keeps them from packing
up and going home. Yet once they have triumphed, they
show no gratitude to him at all and abandon him when he
falls from power.

Mme Mélanie Correur is an unpleasant woman of forty-
eight who had known Rougon in the early days of his
poverty. What she does is shrouded in secrecy, but it is suggested that she is a usurer. She is always urging Rougon
to find sinecures, such as a tobacco concession, for various
bedraggled women, and she even requests, and obtains, a
dowry for a seduced girl who will then be able to marry her
seducer. She herself would like to steal her brother's money,
and we remember her betrayal of Martineau, his death, and
her triumph.

Slightly higher on the political ladder are the members
of the *Corps législatif*. M. La Rouquette is a handsome
young man whose only interests in life seem to be feminine
conquests. There is the pleasant but weak Kahn whose
financial difficulties with the blast furances and the railroad

we have already examined. Finally, there is the silent factory
owner Béjuin, who hangs around scraping up the crumbs
of Rougon's largesse. He is portrayed as never asking
directly for anything, but as always there when something
is offered. He does very well for himself.

On the edge of this sorry collection of individuals is the
uncouth Gilquin, who, like Mme Correur, had known Rougon in adversity. He is the only one who is not desperately
seeking permanment position and bourgeois repectability.
A drunkard, a braggart, and a totally amoral being, he
nevertheless emphasizes by his colorful bohemian qualities
the terrible hypocrisy of all the others. He is, however, no
better than they.

There can be no question that Zola chose these characters
with some care. They represent all classes of society. Gilquin and Mme Correur are essentially of the people, the
d'Escorailles represent the old nobility, the rest are more or
less of the bourgeoisie. In adversity they all hold differing
political beliefs, but when they are getting what they want,
they are Bonapartists to a man. Some are easy-going; others
are harsh and bitter. It does not matter. When self-interest
appears, everything else is forgotten. They are of course dis-
trustful of each other, but can and do act together most of the
time, with such similarity that they give the impression of
terrible sameness. Lulled by their nullity, the reader may tend
to overlook them, keeping his attention fixed on the major
characters who dominate the front of the stage, and he may
not realize the extent to which these low beings dominate
the novel and color nearly every aspect of it, as a chapter-
by-chapter examination will show.

The first chapter reveals that Rougon's clique can pene-
trate into the very hall of government itself. Kahn, Bèjuin,
and La Rouquette are there as deputies, and it is through

them that the preliminary exposition is given. Lest the reader be tempted to believe that we are in the presence of statesmen genuinely concerned with the serious problems of government, Zola quickly disabuses us. Their conversation largely concerns women. As they chat, the other members of the gang take their seats in the spectators' gallery, forming a circle around the legislators below. As Rougon falls, he will have no escape from their continual presence and pressure.

In the second chapter each of them is introduced one by one into Rougon's office as he is packing to leave after his downfall,[66] and Zola gives to the reader the background and desires of each. Again there is a suggestion of military tactics. Despite Rougon's attempt to keep them all out, before long they have infiltrated his privacy, taken over his quarters. The reader is submerged in the details of their individual desires. It is no wonder, then, that in the third chapter Rougon feels the need to escape most of them by visiting Clorinde. But one has the feeling that her exotic apartments provide but a temporary respite for Rougon. Indeed, such is the case, for in next chapter, the scene of the baptism, the leeches reappear. It is the unsavory Gilquin who is the reader's guide to the festivities, as he drags the confused Charbonnels through Paris, with the consequence that the grandeur of the occasion is somewhat lessened. Gilquin sights the Imperial Prince and says: "Houp! C'est le mioche!" (p. 97), and as the baptism takes place, the others all appear on the scene so that by the end of the chapter the official festival has given way to a meeting of the group.

[66] Jouvenel, *op. cit.*, pp. 106-108, states that this scene has a source. Zola was secretary to Glais-Bizoin at Bordeaux when the French government fled there in 1870. Jouvenel suggests that Zola saw the Deputy burning papers as Rougon does. While this is not impossible, we have found no evidence to support this contention, and Jouvenel does not offer any.

But in the midst of the celebration they are all unhappy at
being on the outside with none of the gifts coming to them.
Gilquin closes the chapter on a sordid note by getting drunk.
Thus does their presence lower the tone of the whole chapter.

Except for Rougon's battle with Clorinde in the stable,
the chapter at Compiègne, and the cabinet meeting at Saint-
Cloud,[67] the whole center of the novel is dominated by Rougon's attempts to regain power to satisfy the desires of his
parasites, and then to try to minimize their excesses. Chapters VI and VIII are particularly depressing. To follow a
soirée at Rougon's house would be intolerable had not the
author spared us much of the wearisome dialogue. But the
nation's politics is seen through their eyes, and one example
is instructive to show to what politics can be reduced.

—Oui, je suis bonapartiste, dit-il [Delestang] à plusieurs
reprises; je suis, si vous voulez, bonapartiste libéral.

—Et vous, Béjuin? demanda brusquement M. Kahn.

—Mais moi aussi, répondit M. Béjuin, la bouche tout
empâtée par ses longs silences; c'est-à-dire, il y a des nuances,
certainement . . . . Enfin je suis bonapartiste.

Du Poizat eut un rire aigu . . .

—Je vous trouve bons, vous autres! On ne vous a pas
lâchés. Delestang est toujours au Conseil d'Etat. Béjuin vient
d'être réélu.

—Ça s'est fait tout naturellement, interrompit celui-ci. C'est
le préfet du Cher . . .

—Oh vous n'y êtes pour rien, je ne vous accuse pas. Nous
savons comment les choses se passent . . . Combelot aussi est
réélu, La Rouquette aussi . . . L'Empire est superbe! (pp. 146-
147).

One should add that Du Poizat's criticism is due purely to
the fact that he had not been made a prefect. Had he triumphed with the others, he would not even have thought
of anything critical to say.

[67] Chaps. v, vii, xi.

When Rougon finally regains power in Chapter IX, the group is installed. Zola describes his office:

M. Jules d'Escorailles, qu'il avait pris pour secrétaire, dépouillait la correspondance, sur un coin du bureau. Il ouvrait soigneusement les enveloppes avec un canif, parcourait les lettres d'un coup d'œil, les classait. Devant la cheminée, où brûlait un grand feu, le colonel, M. Kahn et M. Béjuin se trouvaient assis. Tous trois très à l'aise, allongés, chauffaient leurs semelles, sans dire un mot. Ils étaient chez eux. M. Kahn lisait un journal. Les deux autres, béatement renversés, tournaient leurs pouces, en regardant la flamme. (p. 231)

This time, they seem to say, they are there permanently. No other commentary on the political spoils system is necessary.

Even when Rougon makes his trip to the department of Deux-Sèvres to support Du Poizat and Kahn, he cannot escape his captors' pressure upon him. Mme Correur is there to denounce her brother; Gilquin manages to cause his death. But despite Rougon's efforts to help them all, they abandon him for Clorinde when they feel their master weakening. Their final triumph comes when Delestang replaces Rougon in the next-to-last chapter:

C'était la lente prise de possession des familiers, qui baisent les pieds, qui baisent les mains, avant de s'emparer des quatre membres. Et il leur appartenait déjà; un le tenait par le bras droit, un autre par le bras gauche; un troisième avait saisi un bouton de sa redingote, tandis qu'un quatrième derrière son dos, se haussait, glissait des mots dans sa nuque. (p. 374)

This amusing description is more symbolic than realistic. One is reminded of parasitic creepers enveloping a stately tree, rather than human beings actually congratulating a would-be victim. But it is in general true of the novel that in most of the descriptions of the gang, their physical position suggests what they are and what they are doing. It is further

clear, in retrospect, that all their actions have followed a
consistent pattern. They began with a siege, and finally
captured the city, only to move on to the next one when the
captured citadel had been looted. While Rougon and Clorinde dueled in the sun, they remained hidden in the dark.
When Rougon weakened, they swarmed out and were alive
with energy. Their very negative qualities contribute greatly
to the exposition of Rougon's energy, and conversely, their
redoubled energy heightens the other's lassitude.

[Chapter Five]

Zola as a Political Scientist and Historian

Son Excellence Eugène Rougon has not fared very well at the hands of the critics. At the time of its publication, it was largely ignored because *L'Assommoir* had begun to appear in serial form just after the political novel was issued in book form. The resulting storm over the new work made people forget its predecessor.[1] Such reviews as do exist dwell, as usual, on the distortions and excesses of the novelist. For example, "Il a mis dans sa peinture tant de crudité, tant de violence, qu'on se demande s'il n'a pas exagéré."[2] Others hastened to point out that if the Second Empire had its weaknesses, other periods and regimes

[1] Its sale has been fairly modest. According to the catalogue of the Librairie Fasquelle, by 1902 it had sold 36,000 copies; by 1927 (prior to the Bernouard edition), 52,000.

[2] W. Fabrice, *La Vie littéraire*, 23 mars 1876 (cf. LeBlond, p. 429).

did also. "Les Républicians parvenus ont aussi leurs créatures, et ce ne sont ni les moins avides, ni les moins serviles."[3]
As to the first charge, that of exaggeration, we have tried to
show that, regrettable as it may be, Zola has not exaggerated
much. While one can legitimately argue that he carefully
omitted anything which might show the Empire in a favor-
able light, he also refused to exploit many a piquant detail
on the Emperor's escapades, or again, the hopeless confusion
of his Italian policy. As to the second criticism, it can be
said that Zola was well aware that under a Republic, men
remain men. In *La Fortune des Rougon,* while the naturalist is sympathetic to democratic rule, he nevertheless makes
the vile Antoine Macquart a "Republican." But more important, Zola shows the weakness and lack of organization
of the Republicans in the months preceding the seizure of
power by Louis Napoleon; Zola even refers to the paralysis
of the legislature in Paris just prior to December 2 (e.g., p.
111). Later in his career, Zola dissected in *Paris* the many
weaknesses of the Third Republic, and was no less harsh
toward the Socialists, whose constant bickering disgusted
him.[4] Therefore, if he concentrated on the Second Empire in
Son Excellence Eugène Rougon, that does not mean that he
was blind to the defects of other régimes.

There is another, more serious, criticism: that Zola in
exposing the weakness of the Second Empire totally neg-
lected the economic life of the country, the hard work done
by the average person, the vast changes that were taking
place in industry, and above all, the impact that political

[3] *La Revue de France,* t. xviii, avril 1876 (cf. LeBlond, p. 428).
[4] In *SEER,* during a political squabble, Zola states through Rougon
that when five Frenchmen talk politics, there are always five different
governments being proposed (p. 148). Curiously, this same idea is to
be found in the *Journal des Goncourt,* attributed to Hugo (Dec. 27,
1875).

activity and legislation had on the economic life of the nation.[5] We have already mentioned the Emperor's commercial treaty with Great Britian, and the plans for reforestation and agricultural development. There was also the expansion of the railroad system, which according to Rouher's report in 1856 at the Congress of Paris,[6] had been increased by 3,000 kilometers of track since 1852. Later on, the increase would be even more rapid. This Congress is not mentioned in Zola's novel, yet it did indicate the real importance and prestige of France at that time. The suppression of all these aspects of the French political and economic situation distorts the picture; consequently, despite the accuracy of many details, it is asserted that the novel is poor history.

While there is some truth to this criticism, it should be put into proper perspective. First of all, economic history was then in its infancy, and of the few historians who tried to treat it properly, none succeeded very well. Zola's sources were understandably weak on such matters, even Delord, the most reliable and detailed. It was only natural for Zola, whose knowledge of economics was far from overwhelming, to be of his era. Secondly, one must remember that in a certain sense the twenty novels of the *Rougon-Macquart* represent twenty separate chapters of one work. If the political side is emphasized in *Son Excellence Eugène Rougon,* Zola does treat the economic life of the Second Empire elsewhere. *La Curée* shows it at its most venal, *Germinal* at its most poverty-stricken. But in *Au Bonheur des Dames,* Zola is not without appreciation of modern commerce, and finally, in *L'Argent,* he wrestled directly with the problem of capitalism *vs.* socialism. Even in *Son Excellence Eugène Rougon* economic matters are not entirely absent. The chapter con-

[5] G. Lote, p. 84; Hemmings, pp. 58-59.
[6] Schnerb, p. 81.

cerning Rougon's visit to the provinces is no doubt critical and highly mordant. Many projected railroads were not built; others were built at the cost of bribes or for reasons of personal gain, as we have seen. Despite these abuses, Napoleon did much to modernize France by building railroads, and this progress is reflected in the novel. In addition, the Emperor had also a strong belief in agricultural reform, which Zola incorporated into his novel (see p. 182). Napoleon III had written a little pamphlet in 1844 when he was a prisoner at the Fortress of Ham. Entitled *L'Extinction du paupérisme,* the tract showed in great detail what could be done to solve the problem of unemployment and poverty. His idea, not entirely novel, was to establish working communities where all the workers' needs would be foreseen, but where the men would have their own leaders and considerable responsibility. As these poor downtrodden men became rehabilitated as good workers, they might well be siphoned off by industry, but the future Emperor felt that even so, these communities would spread rather than dwindle away. The weakness of his particular Fourier-inspired plan lies primarily in the fact that the least energetic, intelligent, and responsible members of society, all lumped together, are unlikely to create a terrestrial paradise under their own leadership. It is this plan of Napoleon's that is outlined in Zola's novel, and Delestang, owner of a model farm, agrees with the Emperor. Both are vague humanitarian sentimentalists in the eyes of Rougon, who criticizes (p. 182) the whole scheme as impractical, socialistic utopianism, which it was. *He* prefers agricultural communities ruled with an iron hand, and he dreams of reigning over a little kingdom of animals and workers. Zola seems to criticize both attitudes, the authoritarianism of the Minister, as well as the vapidity of the Emperor. It is interesting to note that many years later in *Travail*, Zola's hero Luc Froment considers Fourier's writings as a Bible for economic reform.

Despite Zola's recognition of the new participation by government in the economic life of the country and Napoleon's interest therein, *Son Excellence Eugène Rougon* does take place primarily in the realm of internal politics, isolated from all else. For instance, there is no reference to the Crimean War;[7] the Italian campaign of 1859 is referred to only once (p. 384), and the crucial problem of Italian unity is barely sketched in the last chapter. And, as we have already observed, there is no mention of the Congress of Paris in 1856, nor is there anything about the artistic and literary production of the times. It is of course true that the years 1856-58 and the year 1861 were ones in which foreign events played little direct part. The Mexican adventure had not yet started and Prussia seemed to present no problem. Zola must have been glad that he chose the years in question because his purpose was *not* to paint a broad historical tableau,[8] but to focus his magnifying glass on the mechanism of government, to isolate it and dissect it, as would a naturalist. To succeed in this task, simplification and isolation were necessary.

Zola's analysis of the origins of the Second Empire can be found both in *La Fortune des Rougon* and in *La Curée*. In this latter novel Zola presents the French as being tired of politics, and those who were not tired as being afraid to speak up (p. 60). People had heard enough Lamartinian speeches and had had enough of the ineffectualness of the Parliament. Frightened by the blood of the coup d'état,

---

[7] In the worksheets a minor character, Colonel Jobelin, is indicated as having been in retirement since the Crimean War (*f.* 151), but in the novel he is pictured simply as "retired." Even in *La Curée* which takes place during that war, only passing reference is made (e.g., p. 67) to it. Zola was reserving war for separate treatment.

[8] Despite his statement in the *ébauche* that he wished to do so.

they turned to "les affaires et les plaisirs." This admittedly Republican evaluation, while not original, seems a legitimate one. Zola's second premise—again within the Republican tradition—is that while Louis Napoleon had been legally elected President in 1848, his coup d'état was extralegal and did not represent the continuation of any genuine tradition. The new ruling group was accepted without serious resistance by the nation, out of fear or apathy, and even hailed as a protector of order. But by overthrowing the Republic by a coup d'état, the regime destroyed the orderly procedures for selecting the nation's leaders. Adventurers like Persigny, Saint-Arnaud, etc., influential men in the government, did not have even the indirect approval of the people, and some of these new leaders had not risen through either the legislature or the magistrature. Their sudden appearance meant a lack of continuity in government and a consequent gulf between governor and governed. The official censorship imposed by the Empire further increased the isolation of the ruling circle. It was, therefore, historically legitimate for Zola to situate his novel in this isolated world, for indeed, this vacuum really existed, although not as completely as the novel might lead us to believe. Lest one object that as the Empire developed, new leaders and officials did rise through the legislature, we may point out that until the very end of the Second Empire, the legislature was not really an expression of the people, as the government picked out its own candidates. Although there were some exceptions, it was a body of yes-men who would approve the Emperor's decrees.

What motivated this ruling clique of manipulators can be summed up with the Zola-esque word "appetites." While it may seem an elaboration of the obvious, it is nonetheless necessary to examine closely the reasons and means whereby these hungry men seek to garner power for themselves. Each of these ambitious men wishes to satisfy his hunger, perhaps for power, or perhaps for money or pleasure; but in every case, as in *La Curée,* no one has any interest outside himself—except the Emperor, who does not seem sure of what he wants. There is no attempt to serve any cause greater than oneself. In order to feast at the spoils, however, it is necessary for all to band together and to push one person into a position of authority, because there are not enough jobs at the top. This leader in turn will shower favors on his cohorts and will be obliged to do so, because the moment that he ceases to distribute largesse, his selfish and greedy followers will be transformed from placid leeches into ravenous wolves, ready to turn on him in their search for a more satisfying victim. Such is the case in the novel, when Rougon has no more favors to distribute. But Rougon, too, has an instinct for survival, and swiftly shifts his position to become a member of the Emperor's clique. For this new "loyalty" he is given the job of government spokesman. Thus the nation's government is composed of a series of linked bands of adventurers, starting at the local level in the provinces, each with its leader who is in turn aspiring to be a member of a more important group, all the way up to the Emperor himself.[9]

Hemmings' view of this problem is somewhat different. He summarizes it with this formula: "The strong are supported by the weak," and goes on to consider it "the antithesis, habitual in Zola, between the male and the female

[9] In his notes on Hamel (*f.* 180) Zola mused: "Faire bien sentir dans mon roman l'aventure politique du second Empire, le beau champignon de despotisme qui poussa en France. Rougon ne s'y trompe pas; il s'émerveille, il admire l'aventure, mais il ne compte pas qu'elle aura du succès. Il faudrait des hommes et toujours des hommes, dit-il." The worry seems needless; an endless stream of ambitious men will be ready to start the climb to the top.

principles, the male spurning the female but in the long run at her mercy. Faujas is destroyed by Marthe just as Eugène falls through Clorinde.

"The formula was too diagrammatic to correspond with reality. Statecraft cannot be reduced to a game of beggar-my-neighbour . . . ." (p. 71).

Perceptive as is Hemmings' comment on the sexual undertones of the struggle, the whole problem of the pattern of power may also be viewed in a more traditional manner. Thanks to the clarity with which Zola treated the subject, we are exposed to a fundamentally accurate account of the structure of a Caesaristic regime. We have already mentioned the basic aspects of government by crony and by cutthroat competition; but the naturalist does more than present these obvious matters. He goes into the problem of group relationships in some detail.

When Rougon falls from power in the first chapter, the group's first instinct is to flee to Marsy, but its members suddenly realize that not only does Marsy have his own clique to consider, but also that they themselves are marked as Rougon's henchmen, and are therefore unwanted because "le grand homme" is in disfavor. Therefore, they are finally able to abandon "le gros homme"[10] in the next to last chapter only because Delestang has risen to power from within the group. They are not obliged to combat the members of any other clique. Hence, a wise man (or a stupid one like Delestang, lucky enough to be pushed by the shrewd Clorinde) would come to the realization that in the struggle for power the most effective way is either to attack at the top (like Clorinde) or to work up through one's own channels. Little men, trying to change their allegiance from one op-

[10] "Le grand homme" becomes "le gros homme" when he is out of power or on the way out.

posing group to another, soon may be considered unreliable by all.

Certainly Zola makes it clear that despite the many qualities that the leader may possess, he does not rise to power purely through his own efforts. As the Great Man broods in exile, his small group of henchmen work feverishly in his behalf, for their own aggrandizement. Officers plead with fellow officers, magistrates with other magistrates, all promising spoils in return for support. As Zola puts it: "La bande, dix à douze personnes, tenait la ville" (p. 198). The women are especially useful in converting influential people. If Rougon returns to power after the Orsini attempt, it is thanks to this preparatory work. Thus the drunken Gilquin, who informed Rougon of the assassination plot, can say: "Rougon! c'est moi qui l'ai fait" (p. 95). Zola more than once has a member of the gang use the phrase that the leader must be all-powerful for them to be anything at all (e.g., p. 56). Hence their zeal. The leader's loyalty is clearly, then, a political necessity.

There are other ties that bind leader and follower. Stupid as most of the members of the group undoubtedly are, the leader, seeing them frequently, has grown used to them and they have become a habit with him. Rougon even takes a sort of pride in his imbeciles who all talk politics and pretend to hold various ideological beliefs—pro-Bonapartist when in power, and variously Orleanist, Legitimist, or Republican when deprived of their spoils. Vanity, too, plays an important role. Rougon squirms in anguish when he is unable to help the group which has put all its faith in him. As this lack of power is an admission of defeat (or if one maintains the sexual explanation, impotence), he swears that he will succeed. In short, Zola's analysis, while not subtle, is reasonably elaborate and is based on credible psychology.

It is not too much to say that Zola's examination of these relationships is so detailed because he wished to study the rise to power of Napoleon III himself. In the *ébauche* (*f.* 34) Zola tried to establish various parallels between Napoleon's henchman and Rougon's: "Montrer la bande de Rougon parallèle à la bande du 2 décembre. Clorinde: Morny —le sous-préfet: Persigny—le concessionaire: Billault, le type bohémien—Saint Arnaud—le frère de Mme Rougon: Baroche, etc." These parallels are obviously not good ones, and any direct equation was quickly abandoned as the novel took shape in Zola's mind. But in one case in the final text the original idea does remain as Du Poizat cries out: "Je serai le Marsy de Rougon" (p. 199). These direct comparisons were abandoned, possibly because Zola felt that he could not portray Persigny, Rouher, Baroche, *et al.* historically, for that would deprive him of the freedom of composition that fiction demands. At any rate, Zola created a fictional group, headed by Rougon, that is reminiscent of the historical clique headed by the future Emperor, each seeking a way to arrive at power. Zola established the link necessary to make sure that the reader would not miss the analogy at the time of the cabinet meeting at Saint-Cloud. Here the Emperor suggests that Rougon be more careful in his choice of friends and that he ask for fewer favors.[11] Completely unabashed, Rougon takes out a notebook and reads a request for even more. As the Emperor drily suggests that his friends must adore him, Rougon answers bluntly: "ils ne m'adorent pas, ils me soutiennent" (p. 316). He then goes on to state very pointedly that he trusts that Emperor will

[11] P. 315. Delord, II, 2, points out that "Le gouvernement né le 2 décembre aurait bien voulu se débarrasser des complices qui pesaient sur lui du poids de leur cupidité et de leurs convoitises."

be wise enough to keep with him the faithful servants of the coup d'état, who, he clearly implies, brought Napoleon to power.[12]

It is at this juncture that Zola moves from political theory to history. Did Napoleon's underlings "make" him? The question is not not an easy one to answer, for historians have differed. After the fall of the Empire, the government at Bordeaux explicitly blamed all of the Empire's failings, including the coup d'état itself, on Napoleon III. As for the nineteenth-century Republican historians, they have on the one hand been eager to blame the Emperor personally for having destroyed the Republic, but on the other hand, have wanted to paint him as an indecisive person, swayed by the various individuals around him.[13] Napoleon himself once complained of the lack of unity and support for him at the top, saying that the Empress was a Legitimist, Morny an Orleanist, himself a Republican. Only Persigny was a Bonapartist, and he was crazy. Delord emphasizes the role played by Persigny saying: "M. de Persigny l'arracha presque de vive force à son hôtel de Londres: 'Vous allez me faire fusiller,' lui répétait-il sur le bateau à vapeur qui le ramenait en France."[14] And once in France, prior to December 1848, Louis-Napoleon lived quietly in Auteuil "conseillé par des gens habiles."[15] After his election to the Presidency of the Republic on December 10, 1848, the activity of his able advisors seems to have redoubled. Here it is Hamel who insists particularly on the activities of a small "clique," although not as small as a group of ten or twelve. The "Société du dix décembre" and the "Comité de la rue de

[12] At Compiègne, Rougon had looked up at the lighted window where the Emperor was working late at night, and like Gilquin, had cried out, "Sa bande l'a fait, lui."

[13] Cf. Lote, p. 81.

[14] V, 125.

[15] I, 119.

112   [*Zola's* Son Excellence Eugène Rougon

Poitiers" were working for a violent overthrow of the government.

Le Comité de la rue de Poitiers avait pour lui la richesse et l'influence . . . . Dès les premiers mois de la présidence de M. Louis Bonaparte, ce comité . . . avait ouvert une souscription pour sauver la société . . . . Cet argent (200,000 fr.) fut employé à répandre dans le pays d'infâmes libelles où les doctrines de la démocratie étaient odieusement dénaturées.[16]

Hamel gives an example:

Ecoutez ce petit dialogue tiré du *Manuel du paysan électur*: *Jean* —Mais où veulent-ils [les Républicains] en venir? *Augustin*: Parbleu, c'est bien clair, à mettre la main dans nos poches. —*M. Hardy*: Rien de plus vrai. *Augustin*: Ils prendront encore ta femme à ton nez, et tu n'auras rien à dire.[17]

As for the "Société du dix décembre," its primary concern was to convert the army and the working class: "Aux soldats, aux sous-officiers surtout, elle promettait de l'avancement; aux ouvriers, l'application des doctrines socialistes des livres de M. Louis Bonaparte" (Hamel, p. 180). Later on, in September 1850,[18] it organized a big reception for the Prince-President, going so far as to use strong-arm tactics on those who were not "co-operative." When the group tried to convert the army, it found men like Fleury and Saint-Arnaud ripe for conversion:

Fleury était un ancien viveur, qui s'était engagé après avoir mangé son patrimoine, et qui, en Afrique, avait été protégé par les princes d'Orléans. Au moment de l'élection présidentielle, il se trouvait "un peu sur le pavé de Paris, et au bout de

[16] Hamel, I, 125.
[17] *Ibid.,* I, 126; Delord, I, 155 has the same story, but he says that the pamphlet is Orleanist. Did Hamel cheat? Perhaps so, but at any rate, all the political parties used such defamatory devices. M.A. Romieu's *Spectre rouge de 1852* was one well-known example of an anti-Republican Bonapartist tract.
[18] Hamel, I, 197.

ses pièces." . . . il était allé offrir ses services à M. Louis Bonaparte, lorsque celui-ci n'était encore que simple représentant du peuple.

Zola in his notes for *La Fortune des Rougon*[19] had mentioned this detail, concluding: "Napoléon faisait des généraux pour l'appuyer.—Fleury (mon roman militaire aura un général de cette époque-là)." With such men to help lead the revolution, the rest was not too difficult. Prior to the coup d'état the army was posted in strategic spots in and around Paris; Bonapartist officers held key posts. Republicans were transferred to the provinces. The role of Napoleon himself is hard to estimate. He knew what was happening and had conferences with his henchmen. Hamel contradicts his earlier position when he writes: "Il poursuivait son but, calme, impassible, indifférent aux clameurs méprisantes que soulevait sa conduite tortueuse" (I, 197).

In short, the evidence seems quite clear that Louis-Napoleon was helped to power, which he eagerly desired, by a group of ambitious climbers. The accidental blood-bath of December 4, 1851, was certainly more violent than the future Emperor wished. Events pushed him farther than he desired. Is it not then legitimate to see in Rougon and his group of fictional counterpart to Napoleon and his group? Even as there was bloodshed that Napoleon wished to avoid, so too did Martineau die against Rougon's desires. However, Zola's Napoleon remains in the background, and for this very reason, emerges a more accurate historical figure, as we shall see, than the portrait made of him by the rabid Republican historians.

There have been three fundamental theories concerning the Second Empire.[20] The first is that of a band of adven-

[19] N.A.F. 10345, *f.* 53.
[20] Summarized from Albert Guérard, *Napoleon III* (Cambridge: Mass., 1943), xv-xviii.

turers, including Louis-Napoleon, whose government was
"not a regime, but a racket." The second is based on Bonapartism. As Guérard puts it:

Bonapartism is not Napoleonism: the core of it is not martial
glory, but material order . . . . When anarchy threatens, property demands a strong government and offers the crown to
the most efficient policeman; this is called "saving society."
. . . So the curse of materialism attaches to Napoleon III and
his regime: material order, material prosperity, material pleas-
ures, summed up in the word Bonapartism.

The third, and certainly the least known interpretation
is that of Napoleon III, who considered himself a reformer.

In politics, he stood for Caesarism: democracy incarnated in
one man, a national leader above classes and parties, . . . pledged
to the protection of order, but not of privilege. In the social
and economic field, he held that his first duty to the state was
not so much to defend vested interests or maintain free competition as to improve the condition of the masses. In inter-
national affairs, his aim was friendly cooperation among free
nationalities. His purposes were distorted and thwarted in
application; . . . [but] in eighteen years he achieved much. It
was his hope that humanitarian Caesarism would grow under
the protection of Bonapartism, and ultimately supplant it.[21]
Racketeer, policeman, and reformer, [concludes Guérard] no
student of the period will deny that all three elements were
mingled in that equivocal figure.[22]

Any one of these interpretations taken by itself has certain weaknesses. The serious defect of the first one is that it
fails to take into account the triumphant election of Napoleon
in 1848, before the future Emperor knew any of the "gang"

[21] Delord, I, 512-513 quotes Napoleon's interesting idea that "La
liberté n'a jamais aidé à fonder l'édifice politique durable; elle le couronne
quand le temps l'a consolidé." This idea is mentioned by Zola's Delestang
(p. 312).
[22] Guérard, pp. xvii-xviii.

except Persigny.[23] It also chooses to overlook the question that if France were so despoiled by these looters, how could she arise so quickly after 1871? The weakness of the second concept was that while Napoleon himself certainly stood as a policeman, and had, as we have seen, many plans for improving the country, his henchmen were usually not so scrupulous. Guérard, in his attempt to make as sympathetic a portrait of the Emperor as is possible, is indeed harsh—legitimately—on such men as Morny.

The Napoleonic thesis of reform has, too, its serious flaw. Caesarism means a one-man government that knows what it wants, what the country wants, and has the power to move toward the goal. Unfortunately the Emperor was often indecisive on crucial matters. Above all, because he was in some respects in advance of the thought of his time, and out of sympathy with certain vested interests of his era, he faced constant hostility from those whose support was vital to him, including even his wife. From this uncertainty, as well as from his mistake in reviving a hereditary throne—another contradiction with his basic political beliefs—stems the confusion and the paralysis of the last years of the Empire. These flaws in Napoleon's government are not accidental, and it is of no avail to complain of the bad luck of the Emperor's ill-health. No man is perfect, and one-man government, unchecked, must have the inevitable flaws of its leader. In seizing power illegally and destroying any procedural check, he inevitably brought on an unstable government. Guérard does not, perhaps, stress this weakness sufficiently.

We are now in a position to examine Zola's novel in the light of these differing interpretations. The verdict must

[23] *Ibid.,* p. xvi. This is not literally true. Of course, he knew Morny, but as a matter of fact prior to that date, Morny had had little contact with the future Emperor.

be that, within limits, he chose wisely and accurately. Certainly he adopted the first or racketeer thesis, primarily, but he was careful to concentrate not on the Emperor, but on his subordinates. Here the guilt was only too manifest. As for the second interpretation, Zola borrowed from it, too. He distinguished between the Emperor's sincere desire for order moving towards eventual liberty, and the utter cynicism of the underlings, as exemplified by Rougon's final about-face. As to the final, or Napoleonic idea, with its broad program for economic progress in France and nationalism in Europe, Zola does it less than justice. In *La Fortune des Rougon* and *La Curée,* and later in *L'Argent,* speculation and exploitation dominate; reform is nonexistent. In *Son Excellence Eugène Rougon,* what little we see of Napoleon is critical to some degree, for the novelist stressed the Imperial lust and the weakness of the final years,[24] although this may seem a contradiction. Stressed, too, is the ruthless repression after the Orsini affair. But on the creditable side is the Emperor's personal thoughtfulness, his desire to move, however slowly, in the direction of political freedom. All these traits are historically accurate and justify in theory the idea of Napoleon the Reformer. Zola has avoided any temptation to portray him as a dark villain.[25] Therefore, the pro-Napoleonic Guérard is willing to say of Zola that "his novels may profitably be used, not as authorities, but as illustrations" (p. 323).

It is tempting to accept this idea, that the novel is a

[24] At the cabinet meeting the Emperor seems to forget where he is (p. 301).

[25] Rougon recalls an anecdote about the Emperor, who with blue apron and paper hat, was papering a room for his mistress; Rougon then imagines him cutting out pictures and pasting them in a book (p. 186). If true, it would be senility, not villainy, but Zola makes it clear that in the first instance it is an unreliable anecdote, and in the second, Rougon's imagination at work.

legitimate representation of the government of the Second Empire. One is nearly overwhelmed by the degree to which Zola has faithfully followed historical accounts, and it is easy for the reader's first judgment—that the novel is venomous satire—to turn into the belief that Zola is now an historian. But despite the accuracy of detail and the legitimacy of Zola's over-all historical view of that régime, one is obliged to come to the final conclusion that this novel cannot pass as a fair, balanced portrayal of the Second Empire. We must then ask the question: How can all this history fail to make history?

Zola's method was simple. The novelist consciously limited the scope of his novel so that it did not include the daily lives of the average Frenchman. Any misdeed by any character would therefore do more than merely reflect adversely on an individual; it would immediately put blame on the government, for throughout the book, the characters are continually involved in official functions. They are either seeking office, or seeking to use their office for personal gain. Since every political character in the book is either stupid or grossly immoral, all of the action, all of the history, is seen in the light of the motivations and characters of these people, by whose very presence everything is made cheap, sordid, stupid or evil.[26] It is in this respect that not only Clorinde and Rougon, but also Rougon's henchmen are of great importance in imparting to the book its depressing tone and distorted image.

Another example of this same tone can be seen in the

[26] Guy Robert, *Emile Zola: Principes et caractères généraux de son œuvre* (Paris, 1952), p. 67, puts it as follows: "Il semble cependant que Zola ait manqué son vrai sujet, en éclairant surtout les mesquines intrigues de la 'bande' de Rougon et ses soucis les plus vils; poursuite des bureaux de tabac et des décorations, voire d'un testament à capter. Paraissant dénier à l'art du gouvernement toute complexité et toute dignité, le romancier néglige les questions d'ordre proprement politique."

Orsini affair. In the eyes of historians, the attempt on
Napoleon's life was criminal, but nobly motivated in its
effort to strike a blow for Italian nationalism. The very
severe reprisals taken by the Emperor against the French
people, who were quite blameless in the matter, have been
attributed to his fear that his son might not have any imperial
throne to defend. This is not to justify the attempted assassination nor the actions of a police state, but at least we
are in the presence of historical and personal motives of
some nobility. In Zola's novel the conspiracy is told through
the mouth of Gilquin, and as a result becomes a meaning-
less, sordid tale. The reader remembers little but the details of Gilquin's garret, which he shares with a slut of a
mistress, Rougon's silence on warning the police, Du Poizat's
unspoken suggestion of blackmail, and the sheer joy with
which they all wallow in the power that they seize.

One other example will suffice. We remember that
Rougon's visit to inaugurate the railroad had its counterpart in Rouher's visit to Corrèze in 1863. Certainly Rouher
made his trip as a politician, promising this and that to
keep the region contented. But in the novel, the reader is
aware that he has gone to try to save the skin of his bank-
rupt crony Kahn, and to re-establish the hateful prefect Du
Poizat. Once more, we are given a picture of a society
totally corrupt, led by men whose motives are even more
despicable. They are like dirt on the lens of a camera,
darkening the image that Zola had so scrupulously pre-
served, turning objectivity into polemic under the guise of
truth. This is not perfect history, but one cannot deny that
it is fine satiric art.

[Chapter Six]

Conclusion: The Novel as Art

                      Son Excellence Eugène Rougon
has not been considered one of Zola's great novels. Despite
the fact that the naturalist isolated his world of politics, the
reader does not feel the existence of any "universe" here, to
use the term of Marcel Girard.[1] The great themes of life and
death, birth and decay, do not appear directly as the substance
of the plot and the basis for existence. In Zola's more ele-
mental novels, life and death mean literally that. The struggle for food is a problem in sheer animal survival in *Germinal*
and in *La Terre;* in *Son Excellence Eugène Rougon,* nearly
everything is one step or more removed from the primitive.
If Eugène does not succeed in regaining power at the end

[1] "L'Univers de *Germinal,*" *Revue des Sciences Humaines,* fasc. 69,
1953, pp. 59-76.

of the novel, he can always retire on his income of 30,000 francs as a Senator. There is never any feeling that the members of his group are in genuine want. Hence their struggles are more civilized ones, and we consequently do not feel the overpowering presence of nature. Yet the novel is an absorbing one, and a study of its structure and language may provide some insight into the reasons for this success.

The structure is difficult to evaluate. Upon first reading, it gives the impression of being episodic and fragmented. Our study of the novel's conception and growth shows without any doubt that certain chapters took their existence from the historical requirements of the novelist. Other chapters sprang into place around the first. There is none of the symmetry that characterizes *Germinal,* built around a strike, or of *L'Assommoir,* which shows the simple rise and fall of a family. The chapters are grouped around key events in history, an organization admirably suited to the basic theme that the political world is a never-ending circus with no permanent climax or dénouement. As this idea was basic with Zola in this novel, the structure of the book must be considered artistically satisfying, for in its lack of neat progression, it contributes directly to the vision of the political world, without destroying the continuity of the story and of the conflicts which are at its core.

There is an even more fundamental reason for considering the novel an artistic success. If a nineteenth-century novel may be defined as the struggle of an individual to dominate, or to find a place in, a semistratified society, then Zola's novel is a fair example. Hence, Rougon, the main seeker after power, is the key to the novel's success. We have already showed that Eugène differs from the other characters in the book in that he is endowed with a force and vitality which seem to have their origin in Zola's own desires and temperament. The living power of a man, in Zola's world, is a derivative of the power or powers of nature, which constitutes the source of all energy. As Mlle Antoinette Jagmetti observed in her attempt to arrive at certain aesthetic conclusions on Zola in *La Bête Humaine d'Emile Zola,*[2] the combat between this force and its opposite death, takes place not only between man and nature[3] but within man himself. Life must struggle against inert matter, and as a consequence a dramatic conflict, or tension is created:

Tous ces portraits des personnages les plus différents . . . portent l'empreinte d'un matérialisme lourd et massif. Les descriptions se réduisent à quelques traits, nets, vigoureux, souvent durs. Tout, dans ces visages, est gros, épais, solide; le corps trapu. La matière assume ici encore sa même valeur significative. Les contours précis semblent n'être aussi fortement accentués que parce qu'ils renferment et contiennent les puissances intérieures éruptives et insondables. Toujours prêtes à jaillir, entretenant une sourde inquiétude, celles-ci ne peuvent être retenus et maîtrisées que par les remparts solides de la réalité extérieure.[4]

What is true of *La Bête Humaine* is equally so of Zola's political novel. Here is the description of Rougon when he first appears:

La face tournée vers la salle, avec sa grosse chevelure grisonnante plantée sur son front carré, il éteignait ses yeux sous d'épaisses paupières toujours à demi baissées; et son grand nez, ses lèvres taillées en pleine chair, ses joues longues où ses quarante-six ans ne mettaient pas une ride, avaient une vulgarité rude, que transfigurait par éclairs la beauté de la force. Il resta adossé, tranquillement, le menton dans le collet de son

[2] Geneva, 1955.

[3] One of the most important contributions of Prof. Guy Robert in his *Emile Zola: Principes et caractères généraux de son œuvre.*

[4] Jagmetti, p. 19. This analysis of an individual can also, of course, be applied to a group, for instance, the march of the miners in *Germinal.*

habit, sans paraître voir personne, l'air indifférent et un peu las. (p. 18)

In these few lines, Zola has summed up Rougon's entire development. He is inert matter into which the power of life is suffused, and he becomes alive. But in periods of stagnation or depression, he allows this life to be drained from him, and he sinks back into a mute torpor. In the very first chapter, we see him at his most moribund: "Sa carrure semblait s'alourdir encore" (p. 26). He seems to be sinking back into his own fat, uttering monosyllables, the very picture of inert matter. And yet there is hope for him, because his mind is awake. With one brief comment, he decides the outcome of a discussion. Zola apparently wished to show him at the outset as capable of going in either or both directions.

As the novel progresses, Eugène begins to struggle to regain political power, and it is then that he becomes engaged in combat with Clorinde. Her relationship to him is a peculiar one. It is obvious that they are deadly enemies. She, as woman, is a dangerous and destructive element against which a man must pit his will in order that his force, like Samson's, will not be dissipated through sexual submission. Clorinde appears to him as a constant irritant and a seductive force. When he observes her nude, "Il noua si fortement ses mains, que les doigts craquèrent" (p. 66). But despite the temptation and two lapses of self-control, Rougon never yields to her, for he will never agree to sacrifice his desire to rule to satisfy his momentary pleasure. The extent of his effort is made clear in the following scene, as he tries to conquer his lust:

Il s'était assis sur le canapé, les poings fermés. Un domestique entra l'avertir que le déjeuner refroidissait, sans le tirer de ce recueillement de lutteur, aux prises avec sa propre chair. Sa

face dure se gonflait sous un effort intérieur; son cou de taureau
éclatait, ses muscles se tendaient, comme s'il était en train
d'étouffer dans ses entrailles, sans un cri, quelque bête qui le
dévorait. Cette bataille dura dix grandes minutes. Il ne se
souvenait pas d'avoir jamais dépensé tant de puissance. Il en
sortit blême, la sueur à la nuque. (p. 126)

During these periods of excitement caused by his contact
with Clorinde, his mind, too, becomes stimulated and there
is no mention of the earlier torpor. For this reason, the
adventuress is much more than a piece of window-dressing
for the novel. She is a death-dealing Delilah, but para-
doxically, she is a life-giving source to Rougon as well. She
is, then, both life and death for him as a man; hence his
simultaneous attraction and fear. Both Eugène and Clorinde
are therefore in a state of tension to each other, and Rougon
to himself. Significantly, the fact that Clorinde is not in a
state of tension with herself makes her a less powerful figure.

To heighten the positive effect that Clorinde has on
Rougon, Zola contrasts her with Eugène's legal wife, an
absolutely colorless creature. When Rougon is in her presence, he is always at his most inactive. Their house seems
to be a funeral parlor, and Mme Rougon the undertaker.
Chapter VI begins: "L'été arriva. Rougon vivait dans un
calme absolu. Mme Rougon, en trois mois, avait rendu grave
la maison . . . où traînait autrefois une odeur d'adventure"
(p. 137). Had Rougon remained in that atmosphere, he
would never have awakened sufficiently to return to battle.
He needed Clorinde's exciting presence.

But animal stimulation is not the sole key to Rougon's
activity. Prior to the attempted assassination of the Emper-
or by Orsini, Rougon waits for a break. His torpor is nearly
complete: "Rougon vivait comme une idole indoue, assoupi

dans la satisfaction de lui-même, les mains croisées sur le ventre, souriant et béat au milieu d'une foule de fidèles . . ." (pp. 202-203). The gang is able to revive him only by attacking his vanity, by awakening his thirst for power. When he finally does become Minister of the Interior, his activity is prodigious. He revels in his new job. The more he does, the more he wants to do. He supervises everything. We may then begin to see that he tends to become inactive when deprived of power or the possibility of attaining it, and when not spurred on by his entourage. Conversely, exercise of power increases his appetite.

These same tendencies are visible in the next to last chapter when he falls, thanks to Clorinde's campaign against him. He appears crushed: "Ses muscles de taureau rendaient simplement sa chute plus retentissante" (p. 373). And as the chapter closes, "il sentait davantage cette courbature de tout son être" (p. 380). When he leaves the charity sale and (symbolically) returns to his wife, he decides that as of the very next day, he will take up simpler quarters. Yet at the same time, Clorinde reawakens Rougon's former desire (p. 372), and in defeat he becomes more truly aware of the reality of the situation that he has been in: that is, his power has been less than he thought. Therefore, spurred on by this new awareness, he starts once more (p. 379) to dream of the great things that he will do in the future.

In the final chapter Rougon's will has once again become dominant, and whereas his first elevation to power was aided by Clorinde's dangerous assistance, this time he has freed himself from her completely. As Rougon reaches the peak of his action in the novel,[5] so does the legislature. There is here a peculiar parallel. When Rougon is inactive at the beginning of the novel, similarly, the legislature was

[5] There is no guarantee that he will stay on top.

also dormant by the end of the session. But now, "ce n'était plus le Corps législatif ensommeillé qui avait voté, cinq ans plus tôt, un crédit . . . pour . . . le baptême . . ." (p. 389). This parallel is too close to be entirely coincidental. It is basically the same device that Zola will use later in *La Débâcle* when the human being is symbolically representative (or vice versa) of the society in which he lives. Maurice's fever prior to his death follows the same course as the fires of the Commune that are consuming Paris. Maurice's death symbolizes the end of the era of the Second Empire. Here the parallel is less dramatic, but it exists. Rougon at the height stands for swirling political activity, which had been absent during the authoritarian years of the Empire. Now he and the legislature emerge into the same arena and clash with each other. In this manner Rougon animates yet another part of the novel, so that in the last analysis he is the center of the entire structure. Everyone— Clorinde, his own gang, the Emperor, the legislature—is either pushing him on or combatting him. Hence, he cannot remain dormant.

It is this awakened Rougon who finally hurls himself into society and seizes the spoils. This body of society, by its very nature, is passive and waiting for the arrival of a dominant figure. It is here that the image of the dog bursting through the pack at the *curée froide* at Compiègne shows itself to be central to the novel's vision. During that scene, we remember, the human animal suddenly erupted from behind the façade of civilization. It was night; the torches flickered as in primitive times. The women sniffed the blood of the stag and trembled with pleasure. We were suddenly witnessing, once again, the age-old struggles of life and death, attack and survival, the attempt of life, or action, to conquer death, or inertia. This is Zola's main aesthetic principle: that the force of life is truth and is beauty. In this way, then, he gave his novel that beauty which he considered to be the most basic and meaningful.

Zola was not content merely to erect this framework of general aesthetic principle based on the struggle of life *versus* death. He proceeded to fill in the picture with details of language and situation that elaborate his ideas and provide a richness of tone. It should be said at the outset that Zola's stylistic devices are not very original; they are repeated over and over again in the *Rougon-Macquart* cycle. For this reason an exhaustive analysis of every chapter is not really necessary. But as each of the novels of the series is a different creation, a brief analysis of the main devices will show that the fusion of thought, mood, and language is both typical of Zola's style and particular to the needs of this one work.

The most obvious and well known of Zola's techniques is the description of crowds where the individual is submerged into the mass, where humanity itself is the life force, not the single man. These descriptions always have two main attributes in Zola's novels: noise and motion. In keeping with his central aesthetic of the struggle of life against death, Zola shows that the volume of noise and the degree of motion coincide with the extent to which energy or inertia is dominant. The very first chapter provides a good example. It opens with the *Corps législatif* sufficiently awake to provide a background of sound: "léger tumulte," "brouhaha," which little by little will rise to a great clamor (p. 17). There is also some movement as a few deputies stir about to converse with a colleague. But despite this promise of energy, the dominant note is one of boredom and stagnation. The President of the Assembly speaks "à demi-voix" (p. 7). A secretary's voice is so weak

that he cannot be heard. As the chapter develops, deputies
lower their voices, murmur into each other's ears (p. 13).
This silence is sometimes broken by an occasional strident
laugh and the ringing of the bell calling the Chamber to
order, but these exceptions serve only to reinforce the general impression of lethargy. Likewise, there is little action,
despite the exceptions that we have mentioned above. Most
of the legislators present are motionless in their seats, and
the very paucity of their number symbolizes the weakness
of the group's life-force. At the beginning of the chapter
less than one-half of the members are present, and many of
these are dozing. Zola insists on this somnolence: "som-
meillaient déjà (p. 7); "les dormeurs, étouffant leurs bâil-
lements" (p. 17); "qui s'était assoupi trop profondément"
(pp. 17-18). With sleep goes darkness, and in the best
Romantic tradition, we are reminded that the heavens, seen
through a skylight, reveal "une demi-lune grise, toute la
pluvieuse après-midi" (p. 7). The shadows are dominant
in the hall itself: "Les loges s'enfonçaient pleines d'ombres"
(p. 10). Spectators are lost "dans l'ombre" (p. 15). There
are occasional contrasts to heighten the effect: the white
statues that adorn the hall, the colorful dresses of a few
women present as observers, the green velvet and the gold
picture framing on the paneling. But even the light has
an "éclat sombre" (pp. 7-8).

All during this scene there is a curious insistence on the
inability to see. The secretary on the first page is "myope,"
the hundred deputies have "les yeux vagues," and Kahn
has "les yeux perdus" (p. 8). The spectators who are
present at the beginning of the session have their eyes wide
open but they seem to take in nothing (p. 11). As a final
and clearly intentional detail, Zola ironically presents Mme
Bouchard as ignoring d'Escorailles' advances, and staring,

"sans le regarder," at the allegorical statue of Public Order, which has itself been described as revealing a "face de marbre aux prunelles vides." All of these examples give the definite impression that this absence of sight is intended to represent a lack of force and of awareness of the world. A summary of the vocabulary used in this section shows a concentration of words of attenuation. Verbs: *sommeiller, attendre, se réfugier, murmurer, baisser, s'assoupir, chuchoter, étouffer;* nouns: *chuchotement, balbutiement, ennui, vide, ombre, bâillement;* adverbs: *doucement, négligemment, posément, machinalement, bas;* adjectives: *vide, muet, sombre, gris, monotone.* None of this vocabulary is used in a very startling manner, nor are the words themselves remarkable. It is their accumulation that creates the effect.

This somber world comes to life in the middle of the first chapter. The hall is quickly filled by the members of the *Corps législatif* (239 rather than 100), the noise becomes deafening. The sleeping men wake up, the speaker's voice rings out clearly when he delivers his report, "certains députés exagéraient leur attention, les mains aux oreilles . . ." (p. 20). The spectators, Rougon's clique, lose their vacant stares and follow the proceedings closely. As the climax is reached, motion is introduced when the deputies rush forward from their seats to congratulate the speaker (p. 23). The poor light and bad weather are forgotten. Zola changes his language as he changes the tone. The verbs are now *crier, se précipiter, lancer, rire, jouir, hausser, monter, parler haut;* nouns: *clameur, voix, foule, ravissement, enthousiasme, bravos, flot, débordement, tumulte, remuement;* adverbs: *brusquement, énergiquement, subitement,* etc., etc. Then the mood changes again. After the credits for the baptism have been voted, the majority of the deputies leave (p. 24). The remainder resume their interrupted sleep, the noise drops "comme si le Corps législatif se fût complètement endormi, dans un coin de Paris muet" (p. 24). The legislature, despite this one feverish interlude, is a moribund group. The weather is once more mentioned: "le ciel restait sombre de quelque gros nuage" (p. 27); "La séance . . . se noyait" (p. 27). "Bon Dieu," says the ever-alive Clorinde, "on meurt là-dedans." With this symbolic utterance, she leaves abruptly, waking up the sleeping ushers as she departs.

In like manner Zola wields his descriptive powers in the chapter of the baptism to evoke the life-force of human crowds and to create a symbolic bond between the surging throngs and the brilliant colors of nature. He speaks of the "infini bleu" of the sky (p. 87), as contrasted to the stifling atmosphere inside a building in Chapter I. The June sun is warm and radiant. The clamorous crowd is immense and it shifts constantly like the ocean—"mer de têtes humaines aux flots toujours montants" (p. 88). There is a riot of color, extending from the sunlit towers of Notre-Dame to the red jerseys of the boaters on the blue Seine. Gilquin wears yellow pants, certain marchers in the precession are clad in green. No color is lacking. It would be idle to enumerate all the examples of color. We have only to quote Zola's own summary of the scene: "le cortège entier baignait dans le soleil; les uniformes, les toilettes, les harnais flambaient; les voitures brasillantes, emplies d'une lueur d'astre, renvoyaient des reflets de glace qui dansaient sur les maisons . . ." (p. 100). It is indeed "l'apogée de l'Empire" (p. 107), for in 1856 the Empire was in truth quite energetic.

It would be possible to trace this handling of mass movement in detail throughout the book, but such an analysis would yield only obvious results and add but little to what is already evident in our brief discussion. It would perhaps be of greater value to note that Zola used the same devices not only to portray a crowd, but also individuals. This similarity of treatment is logical within Zola's view of man, whom he regards as a fragment of a group.

We have already examined Rougon's alternating moods of lethargy and action as manifestations of the struggle between matter (death) and the will (life). Zola enriches this central idea with the same profusion of sensory images and experience that he did for the crowd. Rougon enters the *Corps législatif* and slumps into his chair, silent and immobile, seemingly asleep: "Il resta adossé, tranquillement, le menton dans le collet de son habit . . . l'air indifférent et un peu las" (p. 18) and "Il remit son menton dans le collet de son habit, les yeux à demi-fermés, en étouffant un léger bâillement" (p. 19). One may observe Zola's insistence on the fact that he does not see: "sans paraître voir personne" (p. 18); "avant de laisser retomber ses paupières," etc. Rougon never really emerges from his torpor because his resignation has been accepted. At the very end of the chapter, when his clique learns of his fall from power, there is utter silence. During this time Clorinde has shown herself the absolute antithesis of Rougon. She enters noisily. When she sits down in the spectator's gallery, she scans the assembly with her opera glasses. She speaks so loudly that every head turns to stare at her, and finally "voyant que Rougon ne levait pas les yeux, elle tapa à petits coups très distincts sa jumelle sur le marbre de la colonne . . ." (p. 19). At the end of her visit, she leaves in a swirl of silk, again the center of attention.

When Rougon goes to visit her, he who has "sens épais, très longs à s'éveiller," is bombarded with a series of sensual experiences. At the door he meets the servant girl, "qui

mordait dans une orange comme dans une pomme" (p. 61).
"Elle avait les lèvres toutes barbouillées du jus de l'orange."
As Rougon goes up he meets on the stairs a bearded man
"qui le regarda tranquillement, sans lui céder le côté de la
rampe," as if to emphaize by look and deed his dominance
over Rougon. As Eugène arrives at Clorinde's apartment,
the noise characteristically increases: "il entendit grandir
un vacarme de voix, de rires aigus . . . ." When he enters,
La Rouquette is waltzing with a chair to the loud music of
a piano. Clorinde holds court—naked—having her portrait
painted. She poses for Rougon and her sexuality is stressed
in these terms: "le buste renversé à demi, haussant les
pointes des seins, elle souriait, ouvrait à demi ses lèvres,
égarait son regard, la face comme noyée tout d'un coup
dans du soleil. Elle paraissait . . . toute dorée d'un frisson
de désir" (p. 65). Rougon responds to this tableau: "Un
léger frisson venait de lui courir de la nuque aux talons"
(p. 66). The word *frisson* (or certain synonyms: *tressaillement, tremblement, frémissement* and their verb forms *fris-
soner, tressaillir, trembler, frémir*) have a special role in
the novel. The quiver of the flesh appears at certain key
moments, and not only at time of sexual excitement. The
word, as we shall see further, anticipates or announces a
crisis or change from one state of energy to another. Here
we find the paradox that Rougon is awakened by this quiver,
but he is also in danger of being conquered by Clorinde. His
eyes reveal the danger as they lose their ability to see clearly:
"Clorinde, dans ses yeux brouillés, s'élargissait toujours, lui
bouchait toute la baie de sa taille de statue géante. Mais il
battit des paupières, il la retrouva, bien moins grosse que
lui, sur la table. Alors il eut un sourire; s'il avait voulu, il
l'aurait fouettée comme une petite fille" (p. 67). Rougon
has regained his self-control.

The duel between Clorinde and Rougon reaches a climax
in Chapter V. Again Clorinde is surrounded by color,
warmth, and light. Dressed in a blue riding habit, she calls
on Eugène one warm summer day. The sunlight is a
dominant motif: "Elle portait très crânement . . . son chapeau
d'homme, autour duquel une gaze mettait un nuage bleuâtre,
tout poudré de la poussière d'or du soleil" (p. 113). Awakened by her attempted seduction, Rougon's eyes "gardaient
seuls une flamme, . . . et il l'enveloppait alors toute entière
d'un regard" (p. 117). As Clorinde re-emphasizes her de-
sirability, Rougon lowers the blinds ostensibly to keep the
sun from bothering her, but in reality to prepare for his
seduction of her. She objects saying: "Voulez-vous bien
laisser le store! J'aime le soleil, moi, je suis comme dans
un bain" (p. 119). Then as each is fully alive, attempting to
dominate the other, their eyes see clearly: "Elle lui avait
planté ses yeux droit dans ses yeux. Pendant un instant, ils
se regardèrent, si profondément, qu'ils lisaient leurs pensées"
(p. 120). He then suggests that they visit the stable so that
she can examine a new horse that he has acquired. As they go
in, the door bangs shut behind them as if to emphasize the
brusque change from one world to another. We have left
civilization behind, and for the first time in the novel the animal world is literally dominant. It is therefore fitting that the
stable be the scene for the attempted rape by Rougon. It is at
this juncture that olfactory images appear for the first time. J.
H. Matthews has already observed that Zola associates smell
with sex.[6] This correlation is a commonplace in the primitive *Germinal*, but a rarity in the more civilized *Son Excellence Eugène Rougon*. The very first impression that Rougon and Clorinde receive is that of an "odeur forte" (p. 121).

[6] J. H. Matthews, *Les Deux Zola: Science et personnalité dans
l'expression* (Geneva: Droz, 1957), pp. 69-70.

When he attacks her, he begins to sweat: "Il était très rouge maintenant, avec des gouttes de sueur qui commençaient à perler sur ses tempes. L'odeur forte de l'écurie le grisait; l'ombre, chaude d'une buée animale, l'encourageait à tout risquer. Alors, le jeu changea. Il se jeta sur Clorinde rudement" (p. 122). With his sexual excitement, his lips tremble, and Clorinde's eyes take on a gleam of cruelty. The trembling reappears as he calms down after the battle: "De ses mains restées tremblantes, il renouait sa cravate" (p. 124). The odors are no longer mentioned, and when Clorinde finally leaves him, "ses doigts n'eurent qu'un petit frémissement" (p. 125). Later, when he has fully controlled himself, and proposes that she should marry Delestang, "elle ne vit pas tressaillir un pli de sa face. Il avait eu réellement les poings assez gros pour tuer le désir, en deux jours" (p. 130). But sensing that they might at last become lovers without the formality of a wedding, "ils se regardèrent. Pendant un instant, ils eurent un léger tremblement d'hésitation . . . . Ce ne fut, de part et d'autre, que l'abandon d'une minute" (p. 131).

In the sequence of events that we have just examined, the quivers appear when Rougon is trying to dominate Clorinde or is in danger of being dominated by her. The *frisson* shows how precarious his control actually is, even though he finally emerges triumphant over his own flesh, and with his self-control intact. In Chapter XIII we see just the opposite. Rougon's clique is abandoning him; he despairs of ever regaining power. Zola opens the chapter so that the reader cannot fail to sense the mood: "Des semaines se passaient. Rougon avait repris sa vie de lassitude et d'ennui" (p. 197). Heaviness, silence, sleep, lack of sight are once more emphasized: "Dans son salon . . . il faisait ses réussites, pesamment, le nez dans les cartes, sans paraître entendre . . ." and "Lui, au milieu de l'agitation de la bande, semblait ne rien voir." "Ce diable de Rougon vivait comme une idole indoue, assoupi . . ." (p. 202). Then his followers abandon him and he is indeed alone. His distress increases as he visits the Charbonnels, who have given up hope and are returning in defeat to Southern France. As is habitual with Zola, at such a time their room is portrayed as "noire . . . avec . . . des rideaux de damas rouge déteint" (p. 207). The December weather inevitably co-operates: "il fallait venir dans une ville pareille, pour ne pas voir clair chez soi, à deux heures de l'après-midi. Ce jour sale tombant du puits étroit de la cour, c'était Paris. Mais, Dieu merci! il [Charbonnel] allait retrouver le soleil, dans son jardin de Plassans" (p. 207). In this passage the inablity to see (failure to dominate the situation) is openly equated with the gloom of the bad weather.

Rougon convinces the Charbonnels that they should stay in Paris, but his depressed mood stays with him and he meets Mme Mélanie Correur, who reproaches him for his failures. He is soon looking over the parapet of the Seine at the dark green water: "tout se brouilla bientôt, se noya au fond d'une rêverie invincible. Il songeait à des choses confuses, il descendit Mme Correur dans des profondeurs noires" (p. 213). He begins then to dream of emerging from his torpor and of rising again to power. At this moment Zola announces this change of attitude and the forthcoming crisis with "Un frisson le tira de son immobilité" (p. 213). Rougon begins to speculate on what Gilquin's information can be. When the bell rings at home that evening, Rougon "leva les yeux vivement vers la porte" (p. 217). When Gilquin arrives, "il tressaillit" (p. 218). The stage is now set for the story of Orsini's assassination plot and Rougon' subsequent rise to power. And in a beautiful passage at the end of the chapter, Zola describes Rougon walking in the darkness of despair, seeing in the distance the lights of the city, which give him a sense of tremendous power and size. This symbolism foretells Rougon's rise to power, for it is on this very night that the bombs explode under the Emperor's carriage.

Cette soirée d'hiver était très douce, avec un ciel nuageux et bas, qui semblait peser sur la ville, dans un silence noir. Au loin, le grondement des grandes voies se mourait. Il suivit les trottoirs déserts, d'un pas égal, toujours devant lui . . . ; des lumières à l'infini, dans l'enfoncement des ténèbres, pareilles à des étoiles marquant les bornes d'un ciel éteint, lui donnaient une sensation élargie, immense . . . ; et à mesure qu'il avançait, il trouvait Paris grandi, fait à sa taille, ayant assez d'air pour sa poitrine. L'eau couleur d'encre, moirée d'écailles vivantes, avait une respiration grosse et douce de colosse endormi, qui accompagnait l'énormité de son rêve . . . . Il eut un tressaillement, il se tourna, prêta l'oreille" (p. 228).

He thinks that he can hear the explosion of the bombs. He remembers the warm and sunny day of the baptism when he was jealous of the Emperor's glory.

A cette heure, c'était sa revanche, un ciel sans lune, la ville terrifiée et muette, les quais vides, traversés d'un frisson . . . . Lui, respirait à longs soupirs, aimait ce Paris coupe-gorge dans l'ombre effrayante duquel il ramassait la toute-puissance (pp. 228-229).

The key words and ideas that Zola had used from the very beginning of the novel—silence, darkness, emptiness—have been woven into the fabric of the narrative and emerge with dramatic force in this vital scene, charged with all the meaning and power that they possess in a supreme attempt to create a universe for the novel.

But the epic mood cannot be sustained with the structure that Zola gave to his story. Comic satire replaces the grandeur of the preceding chapter, and this alternation of moods continues throughout the work. But if we look ahead to Chapter XIII, we see the sombre mood reappear as Rougon once more falls from power. Leaving the charity sale, where he learns the bad news, he feels "lassitude," and "calme" (p. 379). A rainstorm is about to break, the thunder rolls, the winds blow "et la cime des arbres en gardait un frisson" (p. 379). He returns home in the rain to his silent and empty apartment, to the gray face of his wife. "Au ciel l'orage avait laissé une queue de haillons cuivrés, toute une nuée sale, basse, d'où tombait un reste de jour mélancolique, une lumière louche . . ." (p. 380).

The final chapter shows Rougon once again dominant. It is a warm spring day, "la lumière de la baie vitrée tombant d'aplomb semblait allumer des incendies, dans les orages des grandes séances" (pp. 389-390). And while the statues of Public Order and Liberty still have their empty eyeballs, the mood has changed. Thus "un frisson courut" (p. 393). Rougon had risen to speak. His eyes may be half-closed, but it is only a feint. "Il jeta un regard dans la salle" (p. 393). His voice booms out authoritatively. He triumphs, "rajeuni," and the novel closes on Clorinde's admiring comment: "Vous êtes tout de même d'une jolie force, vous."

Hence we can see that the stylistic devices which support the general aesthetic of the novel are maintained vigorously to the very end. The effectiveness of Zola's language is further enhanced by the fact that its carnal and sensory emphasis fits Zola's physiological and sensory view of man and of the world. Concrete and striking in their visual and auditory power, his descriptions impress themselves on the reader's mind. Thus many pages and even certain chapters are brilliant. But Zola consciously sacrificed the vigor that the novel might have had in order to indulge in low comedy

and satire.[7] Also his overreliance on partially unassimi-
lated historical material gives to *Son Excellence Eugène
Rougon* just a shade of bookishness and of artificiality that
he was unable to dispel. But at its best, the novel resembles
in tone, in details of language, and in stylistic procedure
the greater creations like *Germinal, La Débâcle,* etc. Indeed,
the parallels between *Son Excellence Eugène Rougon* and
the others of the *Rougon-Macquart* cycle are striking: the
original conception preceded the documentation and directed
it, as was to be the case for *La Terre,* and indeed for most
if not all of the twenty-novel series. The structure differs
from that of some of the others novels, but only because the
necessities of the plot differ. The method of composition
was similar. Even the device of splitting the chapter plans
in two can be found elsewhere (cf. *L'Oeuvre*). Again, Zola
never lost sight of the fact that he had intended a portrayal
of the Second Empire, and his satire is as deadly here as
elsewhere. The same themes of corruption and evil are
present as in *Nana* and in *La Curée.* Finally, as we have
just seen, the primordial urge to grasp at existence, to
battle the forces of death, sets in motion this world of Zola's
vision. If the novel cannot be classed with his greatest
creations, it is nonetheless a representative, historically informative, and highly readable chapter in the *Rougon-
Macquart.*

[7] Mallarmé, in a perceptive letter of criticism, March 18, 1876 (in
N.A.F. 24521, *ff*. 462-465) was particularly struck by the comic aspect of
the novel's satire, and wondered whether the humor divorced the story
from reality and created an aura of artificiality.

Bibliography

The following bibliography does not attempt, of course, to be an exhaustive compilation of books and articles pertinent to Zola studies. I have included here only those items that Zola used in his preparation for *Son Excellence Eugène Rougon* as well as any critical book or article that I have cited, or that has directly contributed to this study.

i. *Editions of Zola's Works*

Oeuvres complètes. 50 vols. Ed. Maurice LeBlond. Paris: Bernouard, 1927-1929.

La République en Marche: Chroniques parlementaires. 2 Tomes. Ed. Jacques Kayser. Paris: Fasquelle, 1956.

ii. *Manuscripts of Zola's Notes and Novels*

Manuscript worksheets for *La Fortune des Rougon.* Paris, Bibliothèque nationale: Fonds français, nouvelles acquisitions, vols. 10303-10304.

Manuscript worksheets for *Son Excellence Eugène Rougon.* Paris, Bibliothèque nationale: Fonds français, nouvelles acquisitions, vol. 10292.

Notes et extraits divers. Paris, Bibliothèque nationale: Fonds français, nouvelles acquisitions, vol. 10345.

iii. *Unpublished Letters to Emile Zola*

MALLARMÉ, STÉPHANE. Letter to Zola. Paris: Bibliothèque nationale: Fonds français, nouvelles acquisitions, vol. 24521, *ff.* 462-465.

Ten Brink, Jan. Correspondence with Zola. Paris: Bibliothèque nationale: Fonds français, nouvelles acquisitions, vol. 24512.

IV. *Books Consulted*

Alexis, Paul. *Emile Zola: Notes d'un ami.* Paris, 1882.

Bac, Ferdinand. *La Cour des Tuileries sous le second Empire.* Paris, 1930.

———. *Intimités du second Empire: la cour et la ville.* Paris, 1931.

Beaumont-Vassy, Vcmte de. *Histoire initime du second Empire.* Paris, 1874.

Décaux, Alain, *La Castiglione: Dame de cœur de l'Europe.* Paris, 1953.

Delord, Taxile. *Histoire du second Empire (1848-1869).* 6 vols. Paris, 1869-1875.

Dhormoys, Paul. *La Cour à Compiègne: Confidences d'un valet de chambre.* Paris, 1866.

Doucet, Fernand. *L'Esthétique d'Emile Zola et son application à la critique.* Paris, 1923.

Fleury, le Grl. *Souvenirs du général comte Fleury.* Paris, 1898.

Guérard, Albert. *Napoleon III.* Cambridge, Mass., 1943.

Halévy, Ludovic. *Carnets.* 2 vols. Paris, 1935.

Hamel, Ernest. *Histoire Illustrée du second Empire, précédée des événements de 1848 à 1852.* 3 vols., 2 tomes. Paris, 1873-1874.

Hemmings, F.W.J. *Emile Zola.* Oxford, 1953.

Hermant, Abel. *La Castiglione, la dame de cœur des Tuileries.* Paris, 1938.

Hoche, Jules. *Les Parisiens chez eux.* Paris, 1883.

Jagmetti, Antoinette. *La Bête humaine d'Emile Zola: Etude de stylistique critique.* Geneva, 1955.

Journal des Goncourt. 20 vols. Ed. Ricatte. Monaco, 1956.

Jouvenel, Bertrand de. *Vie de Zola.* Paris, 1931.

Laporte, Antoine. *Le Naturalisme ou l'immoralité littéraire.* Paris, 1894.

Loliée, Frédéric. *Les Femmes du second Empire.* Paris, 1954.

MATTHEWS, J. H. *Les Deux Zola: Science et personnalité dans l'expression.* Geneva, 1957.

Papiers et correspondance de la famille impériale. Tome 1. Paris: Imprimerie nationale, 1870.

PRADALIÉ, GEORGES. *Balzac Historien.* Paris, 1955.

ROBERT, GUY. *Emile Zola. Principes et caractères généraux de son œuvre.* Paris, 1952.

————. *La Terre d'Emile Zola.* Paris, 1952.

ROMIEU, AUGUSTE. *Le Spectre rouge de 1852.* Paris, 1851.

SCHNERB, ROBERT. *Rouher et le second Empire.* Paris, 1949.

TAISEY-CHATENOY (pseud. for IRÈNE DE GENGOUX, MARQUISE DE). *A la Cour de Napoléon III.* Paris, 1891.

VIEIL-CASTEL, HORACE DE. *Mémoires sur le règne de Napoléon III (1851-1864).* Paris, 1883-84.

WILSON, ANGUS. *Emile Zola: An Introductory Study of His Novels.* New York, 1952.

XAU, FERNAND. *Emile Zola.* Paris, 1880.

v. *Critical Articles*

AURIANT, L. "Emile Zola et les deux Houssaye. Documents inédits," *Mercure de France,* CCXCVII, June, 1940, 555-569.

GIRARD, MARCEL. "L'Univers de *Germinal,*" *Revue des sciences humaines,* fasc. 69, 1953, pp. 59-76.

GRANT, ELLIOTT M. "Studies on Zola's *Son Excellence Eugène Rougon,*" *Romanic Review,* XLIV (1953), 24-39.

KEINS, JEAN-PAUL. "Der Historisches Wahrheitsgehalt in den Romanen Zolas," *Romanische Forschungen,* XLVI (1932), 361-396.

LOTE, GEORGES. "Zola, historien du second Empire," *Revue des études napoléoniennes,* juillet-août, 1918, pp. 39-87.

RAPHAËL, PAUL. "*La Fortune des Rougon* et la vérité historique," *Mercure de France,* Oct. 1923, pp. 104-118.

Index

In this index, the names of fictional characters have been set in capital and small capital letters.